WHEN YOUR DAYS ARE DARK,

"Gary Zimak's treatment of suffering moved me as caregiver to my husband, who has a chronic illness. Through scripture, Zimak illustrates how God uses everything for good, shining the light of hope in the recesses of despair. This book is a powerful reminder that, even in the depths of suffering, God is good, all the time."

Maria Morera Johnson
Author of *My Badass Book of Saints*

"In a fallen world, we all have our dark moments. Faith can be challenged at such times, which is why we need practical wisdom and encouragement. Gary Zimak always delivers and never disappoints. This book is a timely resource for us all. If times are good, it can help prepare us. If times are dark, it can help us persevere. I strongly recommend this book!"

Fr. Jeffrey Kirby
Author of *Be Not Troubled*

"This book offers hope, not pat answers. Looking at the suffering people endured in stories from scripture, it will spark your imagination to consider how God was present then—and how God is present now in the midst of your own suffering. This book reminds us that we are never alone."

Deacon Ed Shoener
Coeditor of *When a Loved One Dies by Suicide*

BIBLICAL ADVICE
TO HELP YOU TRUST
IN DIFFICULT TIMES

WHEN YOUR DAYS ARE DARK,

God Is Still Good

GARY ZIMAK

Ave Maria Press, Notre Dame, Indiana

Scripture quotations are from the *Revised Standard Version of the Bible—Second Catholic Edition (Ignatius Edition)*, copyright © 2006 National Council of the Churches of Christ in the United States of America. Used by permission. All rights reserved.

© 2023 by Gary Zimak

All rights reserved. No part of this book may be used or reproduced in any manner whatsoever, except in the case of reprints in the context of reviews, without written permission from Ave Maria Press®, Inc., P.O. Box 428, Notre Dame, IN 46556, 1-800-282-1865.

Founded in 1865, Ave Maria Press is a ministry of the United States Province of Holy Cross.

www.avemariapress.com

Paperback: ISBN-13 978-1-64680-188-6

E-book: ISBN-13 978-1-64680-189-3

Cover image © iStock / Getty Images Plus / Massimo Pollani.

Cover and text design by Samantha Watson.

Printed and bound in the United States of America.

Library of Congress Cataloging-in-Publication Data is available.

CONTENTS

Introduction **vii**

1. What Was Paul Thinking? **1**
2. When We Mess Up (Adam and Eve) **13**
3. When God Is Late (Lazarus) **21**
4. When Others Mess Up (Joseph) **29**
5. When Bad Stuff Happens (Ruth and Naomi) **39**
6. When Your Dream Falls Apart (Disciples on the Road to Emmaus) **49**
7. When You've Been Used, Rejected, or Abandoned (Hagar) **59**
8. When You're Not Strong Enough (Paul) **67**
9. When You're Persecuted for Your Faith (Shadrach, Meshach, and Abednego) **75**
10. When You're Hiding in Fear (Apostles in Upper Room) **85**
11. When You've Made a Bad Decision (Jonah) **93**

12. When There's No End to Your Suffering (Woman with a Hemorrhage) **101**
13. When You're Struggling Financially (Elijah and the Widow) **109**
14. When You're Grieving the Death of a Loved One (Widow of Nain) **119**
15. When You Just Don't Understand (Job) **129**

Conclusion: Believing Is Seeing **137**

Introduction

> We know that in everything God works for good with those who love him, who are called according to his purpose.
>
> —Romans 8:28

For those seeking consolation in the pages of the Bible, it generally doesn't take long to discover this verse. When it comes to explaining the "unexplainable," I can't think of another verse that is used more often than this one. The message behind this verse is that no matter what happens in life—death, sickness, betrayal, financial ruin, or any catastrophic event—God can bring good out of it. It's a great message and is easy on the ears, but is it really true?

I believe with all my heart that the sentiment expressed in this Bible verse is 100 percent true. In my opinion, however, those who are grieving or distraught need something more, and that's why I wrote this book. Even though I have included this verse in many of my talks and books, I felt it was time to go deeper. Posting this verse on social media or using it as part of a pretty wall hanging may be enough to inspire those who are dealing with the ordinary struggles of life, but it's not going to be enough for the mother whose child just died from suicide, the husband grieving the sudden death of his wife, or the individual who just lost everything in a natural disaster. It may sound good to many, but not to someone who just suffered a devastating loss. That individual needs something more than a Bible verse hanging on the wall. They need proof that these words are true.

I have authored twelve books, and this is by far my most challenging project. It's the book I was always afraid to write, but the one I knew had to be written. I've spent more than ten years speaking and writing about breaking free from worry by establishing a close relationship with Jesus. In that time, I have met hundreds of people who were struggling to find God in the midst of inexplicable circumstances. You may be in this category right now, or maybe you have been there in the past. If not, you will almost certainly be there in the future. I wrote this book for you.

WHAT TO EXPECT IN OUR JOURNEY TOGETHER

There have been other authors who attempted to tackle this topic, but I believe that my approach is unique. Before I committed to writing this book, I decided not to address suffering by speaking about potential "silver linings." Instead, I chose to dig into scripture and conclusively show

Introduction

how God works in tragedy and chaos. I wanted readers of this book to see beyond a shadow of a doubt that God is active in the messiness of life. My hope is that once you see how the Lord was working "behind the scenes" in these events from the Bible, you'll be more inclined to believe that he's doing so in your life as well.

I have also made a conscious decision to avoid answering the "why?" question for the simple reason that none of us knows for sure why God does what he does. Rather, I'll focus on the "what," "how," and "where" of his work in the lives of his people throughout the ages. Pointing out what he has done and the good that resulted will allow you to draw your own conclusions about your unique circumstances. I hope that it will also bring you comfort even when you don't have all the answers.

Here's how the book works. We'll start by unpacking Paul's radical assertion that God uses all circumstances to express his love for us. Then, we'll take a look at Paul's life and search for insight into how he felt confident in making such a bold claim. We'll learn how the Holy Spirit can help us to see God working in the messiness of life. We'll look at Paul's teachings about the imperfect nature of this world and why we can confidently expect things to get better. And we'll learn how to pray through all of this in a way that leads to peace and acceptance.

Then we will examine several biblical examples of God working in seemingly horrendous situations. Some of the stories will be familiar and others will be obscure, but a constant theme will emerge: God really can bring good out of anything. As I mentioned previously, the examples we look at will offer definitive proof of God's involvement.

Each chapter will also contain discussion questions and a prayer. I urge you not to skip over them. The questions will help you tie the material to your personal situation, and the prayers will bring you into contact with the Lord and allow him to intervene in your life.

Do you believe that God can bring good out of any situation? It's okay if you don't. That's why I wrote the book. Even though I believed it when I started this project, examining and writing about these real-life stories caused my confidence level to grow even more. I believe strongly that the same thing will happen to you.

IS IT WELL WITH YOUR SOUL?

Horatio Spafford was a successful attorney and real-estate investor who lost much of his fortune in the Great Chicago Fire in 1871. Two years later, his family scheduled a much-needed European vacation. When the time for departure came, Horatio was tied up with business matters, so his wife and four children sailed without him. He planned to join them a few days later. On November 22, 1873, their ship was struck by an iron sailing vessel, and all four of his daughters died. Only his wife survived. While sailing across the Atlantic to meet her,

Horatio Spafford penned the words to the classic hymn "It Is Well with My Soul." The song begins with the following words:

> When peace like a river attendeth my way
> When sorrows like sea billows roll
> Whatever my lot, Thou hast taught me to say
> It is well, it is well with my soul.

In the midst of an unthinkable tragedy, Horatio Spafford was somehow able to recognize God's presence and be filled with his consolation. He may not have understood why things unfolded the way they did, but he was filled with the hope he needed to move forward.

No matter how bad things look in your life right now, I can confidently assure you that God's plan for good is falling into place. How that manifests itself in your life remains to be seen. My expectation is that, after reading this book, you'll be able to see his providential care at work. Let's begin with a brief prayer, confident that God will hear and answer us.

PRAYER

Heavenly Father, as I begin this book, I acknowledge the fact that things are happening in my life and in the world that I don't understand. I know that you love me, but in all honesty, it doesn't

seem like it sometimes. Please pour out your
Spirit into my heart so that I can better see your
hand in everything that happens in my life. I ask
this in the name of Jesus. Amen.

Chapter 1

WHAT WAS PAUL THINKING?

Because this entire book is based on the concept that God can bring good out of all things, let's begin by examining the basis for that theory from Paul's Letter to the Romans: "We know that in everything God works for good with those who love him, who are called according to his purpose" (8:28). This is one of the most comforting yet perplexing verses in all of scripture. Throughout this book, we will look at examples of this incredible assertion in action, but first let's look at the message itself, phrase by phrase. What exactly was Paul saying when he wrote these words to the Church in Rome some two thousand years ago? And how should we read them today?

"WE KNOW . . ."

Paul begins with the confident proclamation that what he's about to write is true. Before even considering the content of the verse, it's important to recognize the absolute certainty that prefaces what he is about to say. We all know that the sky is blue and that cherries are red, but not everyone knows that God works in both the pleasant and unpleasant happenings of life. Despite all the adversity and suffering Paul faced, he knew this to be true.

Considering the importance of what he was about to say, I'm glad that Paul didn't open this verse with the words "we think" or "we hope," as that would have left an opening for doubt to creep in. There's no mistaking the mindset of someone who begins a statement with the words "we know." *We* might not know, but *he* does—all the more reason to pay attention to his words.

"IN EVERYTHING . . ."

For a believer, it doesn't take much to see God's hand in the good things of life—a job promotion, good health, a new baby, financial gain, or a sunny day. He often gets credit, as he should, for bringing these things about. But while it's true that God is involved in all of life's pleasant happenings, he also has a hand in all of the not-so-pleasant things as well.

The same God who produces warm, sunny days is also responsible for days filled with clouds, rain, and wind. And, when you think about it, isn't that the way it should be? Otherwise, we'd be faced with the reality that God abandons us in times of trouble. He doesn't. In sunshine and in rain, he is always working to help us.

"GOD WORKS FOR GOOD . . ."

The fact that God works in all things doesn't mean that all things are good. Such things as murder, adultery, or violence are not good. They are evil, and the fact that God can bring good out of them does not make them good.

Here's how the *Catechism of the Catholic Church* explains it: Even though God can bring good out of evil, evil itself is never a good (*CCC*, 331). To take the most dramatic example, the greatest evil was our rejection and murder of God's only Son. From that evil, God brought the greatest of goods—the Resurrection of Christ and our redemption. But even that reversal didn't change the evil of Christ's betrayal and death into something good in itself. Instead, God used the occasion of evil to bring forth good. The fact that not all things are good doesn't stop God from bringing good out of them. He can and he will, if we let him.

"WITH THOSE WHO LOVE HIM . . ."

At some point we have to consider the ultimate "good" any of us could ever experience—eternal life in heaven. There is no greater good. When looking at Paul's proclamation, it's important to keep this in mind. There will be pain and suffering in life, but it's all designed to bring us our greatest good: union with God forever.

It is essential to remember that God allows us to participate in his plan. That's what Paul is getting at when he singles out "those who love him." Christian love is not a feeling, but rather a conscious decision. Yes, God can and will work good in our lives, but we can stop him from doing so. How? We do it mainly by refusing to acknowledge and obey him—in other words, by not loving him.

"WHO ARE CALLED ACCORDING TO HIS PURPOSE"

We're not always aware of it, but God has a plan for each of us. That plan is for us to enter into a relationship with him in this life and spend eternity with him in heaven. He arranges the circumstances in our lives to give us the best possible chance for that to happen. It's not easy to accept, but that plan sometimes involves trials and suffering.

We are called by God. He loves us unconditionally and wants us to love him in return. In order to do that, however, we'll have to accept some things that are difficult to accept. It will take work to get to the point where, like Paul, we'll know for sure that everything that happens can draw us more deeply into God's love. What better place to begin than by examining the life of the man who truly believed that God works in all things for good.

WHO WAS PAUL?

In chapter 7 of the Acts of the Apostles, in the midst of the arrest and murder of a deacon named Stephen, we are first introduced to an unsavory individual by the name of Saul. Not only did this young man consent to the brutal stoning of Stephen, but he entered multiple Christian households, dragging men and women into prison. It may seem unlikely to us, but this notorious persecutor of Christians would be the person handpicked by God to deliver the Gospel message to non-Jewish people. Better known by his Roman name of Paul, this persecutor-turned-apostle is the person responsible for the theme of this book.

As is often the case, it took some serious divine intervention to get Paul from point A to point B. As he was traveling on the road to Damascus to capture more Christians, Paul had a life-changing encounter with Jesus Christ. While scripture doesn't support the often-stated claim that he was knocked from his horse, Paul did experience something that turned his world upside down. After being questioned by Jesus ("Saul, Saul, why do you persecute me?" [Acts 9:4]), Paul was blinded and told to enter the city and wait for further instructions. He obeyed. This is the first example of God using adversity in Paul's life to accomplish great things, but it wouldn't be the last.

As detailed throughout the New Testament, Paul would go on to be shipwrecked, imprisoned, beaten, and rejected. Amazingly, he never let any of these struggles stop him from proclaiming the Gospel. If anything, he drew strength from his suffering and viewed it as a way to build character and share in the mission of Christ. Here's how Paul described his relationship to suffering:

> More than that, we rejoice in our sufferings, knowing that suffering produces endurance, and endurance produces character, and character produces hope, and hope does not disappoint us, because God's love has been poured into our hearts through the Holy Spirit which has been given to us. (Rom 5:3–5)
>
> Now I rejoice in my sufferings for your sake, and in my flesh I complete what is lacking in Christ's afflictions for the sake of his body, that is, the church. (Col 1:24)

Ultimately, Paul's desire to serve Christ and be led by the Holy Spirit enabled him not only to accept suffering, but to rejoice in it. The trials he endured and the accompanying grace provided by the Lord eventually allowed Paul to see something we often miss: God can bring good out of suffering.

To me, this is the ultimate message of hope. More than anything else, I want to believe that God is in control of my life. Embracing this philosophy enables me to wake up each morning knowing that nothing happens by accident. Even when free will and poor choices cause "unfortunate" events to occur in my life, I want to take comfort in the fact that God is still in control. For that reason, I find a great deal of hope in the life of Paul and his assertion that God brings good out of all things if we let him.

Now, before you get discouraged and think that Paul is so far out of your league that you'll never be able to trust God like he did, I have some good news for you. Even after his encounter with Jesus on the road to Damascus and his subsequent conversion, Paul knew what it was like to feel hopeless:

> For we do not want you to be ignorant, brethren, of the affliction we experienced in Asia; for we were so utterly, unbearably crushed that we despaired of life itself. Why, we felt that we had received the sentence of death; but that was to make us rely not on ourselves but on God who raises the dead; he delivered us from so deadly a peril, and he will deliver us; on him we have set our hope that he will deliver us again. (2 Cor 1:8–10)

Although the details of this incident are vague, Paul makes it clear that he was in a bad place. Look closely at his overall message, however. Being on the verge of despair taught him to rely not on himself, but on God. Furthermore, the fact that God came through in this time of great suffering enabled Paul to face the future with confidence.

LESSONS FROM ROMANS 8

It may take time, but you can begin to see suffering in a different way. In order to help you get started, let's take a brief look at some of the other points Paul made in chapter 8 of his Letter to the Romans.

Life in the Spirit

Paul emphasizes the importance of living in the Spirit, not in the flesh. To set your mind on the Spirit brings life and peace. As taught by the Church and stated by Paul in Romans 8:9, the Spirit dwells in those who are baptized. And because the Holy Spirit is the Spirit of Christ, this gift of the Spirit can help us to see things from Christ's perspective. The world may see the bad in a situation, but Jesus can see the good. Therefore, the Spirit gives us the ability to see situations as Jesus did—through God's eyes.

This Isn't Heaven

In Romans 8:18, Paul reminds us of something self-evident: there is suffering in this life. Any denial of that fact is simply not realistic. Paul takes some of the sting out of that admission by proclaiming that any suffering we experience in this life *isn't even worth comparing* to what awaits us in our heavenly home. In order to appreciate this fact, however, it's necessary for us to cultivate the virtue of hope. Doing so allows us to look past any suffering we encounter, recognize its temporary nature, and look forward to a day when suffering will be no more.

Praying in the Spirit

In Romans 8:26, Paul acknowledges that sometimes we don't know what to pray for, especially when we encounter a difficult challenge or extreme suffering. When faced with suffering, my first inclination is to pray that it goes away. While there's nothing wrong with doing that, there are times when the suffering remains and is drawing me to a greater good. I may not be able to see it, but the Holy Spirit does. That's when the Spirit can help us to pray for what we really need.

God's Love in Action

As the eighth chapter of Paul's Letter to the Romans draws to a close, he leaves us with a piece of information that is woven throughout the pages of this book. Any suffering that we encounter in life can become an occasion for us to more deeply experience God's love for us. It's a difficult concept to accept, but one that goes a long way in reconciling suffering with God's love. No matter what we experience in life, God is expressing his love for us, in all circumstances we face:

> Who shall separate us from the love of Christ? Shall tribulation, or distress, or persecution, or famine, or nakedness, or peril, or sword? . . . No, in all these things we are more than conquerors through him who loved us. For I am sure that neither death, nor life, nor angels, nor principalities, nor things present, nor things to come, nor powers, nor height, nor depth, nor anything else in all creation, will be able to separate us from the love of God in Christ Jesus our Lord. (Rom 8:35, 37–39)

In the chapters that follow, we'll look at people whose lives prove the truth of Paul's statement that "in everything God works for good." Undoubtedly, Paul was familiar with many or all of these stories, especially the ones documented in the Old Testament, so I don't think it's a stretch to conclude that his thinking may have been influenced by some of them. If they could influence him, they can have a similar effect on each one of us, too. God really can bring good out of any situation, but don't just take my word for it (or Paul's, for that matter). Let's look at some real-life examples.

PRAYER

Dear Jesus, I could definitely use your help in understanding the value of suffering. So many things just don't make sense to me. Based on your experience in the garden of Gethsemane, I know you can relate. You weren't anxious to suffer, but you knew it was necessary. Thank you for giving me such a good example, but I'm going to ask for more. Please change my heart so that, like you, I desire nothing more than doing the will of the Father. Amen.

DISCUSSION QUESTIONS

1. What situation in your life do you find the most difficult to see as an expression of God's love? Say a quick prayer to the Holy Spirit ("Come, Holy Spirit!"), and then try to think of any potential good that could come out of this situation.

2. Why do you think Paul was so confident about his belief that God can bring good out of any situation?

3. In your opinion, what is the key to finding peace in the difficulties of life? What is necessary to reconcile the idea of an all-loving and all-powerful God with tragedy and suffering?

Chapter 2

WHEN WE MESS UP (ADAM AND EVE)

Genesis 2:7–3:24

One of the most disheartening situations we can experience involves messing up a good thing with no hope of reparation. I first experienced this kind of hopelessness as a child, and I have revisited it dozens of times over the years. Whenever I mess things up, my head is filled with an endless series of thoughts: *If only I didn't say or do that. Everything was fine until I ruined it. Now my life is a disaster, and there's nothing I can do to repair the damage I caused.* Being immersed in this kind of regret, shame, and despair is not a good place to be. Adam and Eve were the first humans to go through it, so let's look at their story.

THE FACTS

Adam had a good thing going. Created by God to live with him in paradise, the first man lived in a state of friendship and harmony with God. According to the *Catechism of the Catholic Church*, "The first man was not only created good, but was also established in friendship with his Creator and in harmony with himself and with the creation around him, in a state that would be surpassed only by the glory of the new creation in Christ" (*CCC*, 374). Adam was given just one basic instruction from God: "And the Lord God commanded the man, saying, 'You may freely eat of every tree of the garden; but of the tree of the knowledge of good and evil you shall not eat, for in the day that you eat of it you shall die'" (Gn 2:16–17). As good as things were for Adam, the Lord wanted to make it even better. Recognizing that it wasn't good for the first man to be alone, God created Eve. The couple was now able to enjoy each other's company in addition to the fruits of the garden. At this point, suffering and death were still not in the picture. It was a best-case scenario, appropriately known as paradise.

The only thing that could have caused Adam and Eve's perfect happiness to come to an end was their disobedience to God. This gave the serpent an opening to stir up some trouble. Choosing to approach Eve, the serpent planted seeds of suspicion in her mind by telling her that God was lying with the "eat from this tree and you will die" threat. After contemplating his words, Eve looked at the attractiveness of the tree and concluded that eating from it would make her wise, so she gave in and helped herself to some of the forbidden fruit. She also gave some to Adam, who ate it as well.

The actions of Adam and Eve caused death to enter the world and broke the union with God that we were created for. Realizing that they did something wrong, they attempted to hide from God in the garden. Even if they didn't fully understand the long-range effect of their disobedience, the fact that they hid from God indicates that they had some awareness of their wrongdoing.

Fortunately for them and for us, our God is a God of second chances. Even though Adam and Eve tried to place the blame elsewhere (Adam blamed Eve and Eve blamed the serpent), the Lord made clear that he planned to fix the damage caused by their disobedience. Speaking to the serpent, he said, "I will put enmity between you and the woman, and between your seed and her seed; he shall bruise your head, and you shall bruise his heel" (Gn 3:15). The *Catechism* elaborates:

> After his fall, man was not abandoned by God. On the contrary, God calls him and in a mysterious way heralds the coming victory over evil and his restoration from his fall. This passage in Genesis is called the *Protoevangelium* ("first gospel"): the first announcement of the Messiah and Redeemer, of a battle between the serpent and the Woman, and of the final victory of a descendant of hers. (*CCC*, 410)

God didn't go into a lot of detail, but from the very beginning, he indicated that he planned to somehow repair the damage caused by the disobedience of Adam and Eve.

A CLOSER LOOK

Adam and Eve were definitely living the good life. They had everything they needed to make them happy, but somehow it wasn't enough. Exploiting the situation, the serpent came along and convinced Eve that God was holding out on them. Believing his lie, she decided to disobey God and convinced Adam to do the same. Not only did their disobedience affect them, but they set a trajectory for all future generations. If one was to compile a list of all-time bad decisions throughout history, this one has to rank at the top of the list. No matter how you look at it, this was a really bad situation. Even though they both tried to pass the buck, Adam and Eve were ultimately responsible for the mess they created.

Because God is merciful, however, he wasn't about to abandon his children. He had a plan. Even though it would take thousands of years to play out, he would send a Messiah to undo the disobedience of Adam and Eve. It was a complicated plan that would involve many additional missteps (King David's sinfulness immediately comes to mind), but it would fulfill his promise first spoken to the serpent in the presence of Adam and Eve.

When reading this story, it's very easy to immediately ponder, "What if?" or "If only . . ." or "Why did God let it happen?"—but that type of toxic thinking is useless. It also puts limits on God and ignores the important truth that he can always bring something good out of our mistakes. As the case of Adam and Eve illustrates, the Lord specializes in working with the broken pieces created by his imperfect children.

Something else to consider when looking at this story is God's schedule. Even though he would go on to fix the mess caused by Adam and Eve's disobedience, he didn't do it in their lifetime. It took thousands of years for the Messiah to be born and repair the rift between God and humanity. Furthermore, the way that the damage was repaired seems radical. Why was it necessary for Jesus to be crucified, and why was there such a long wait? Only God knows the answers to those questions. Rather than try to figure out his ways, it's more productive to look at the results. Adam and Eve caused the problem but couldn't fix it. In his mercy, God stepped in and repaired the damage.

Even though this story has a happy ending, it teaches us an important lesson: our actions have consequences. Even though God is all-powerful and can do anything he wants, he didn't remedy this situation by turning back the hands of time or totally cleaning up the mess. Even though the rift has been repaired, we are still affected by Adam and Eve's disobedience. Sickness and death, for instance, came about because of their disobedience. God certainly worked wonders with the mess they created, but he chose to let many of the consequences remain.

WHY IT MATTERS

Throughout my life, I have struggled to believe that God can clean up after me and turn my mess into something good. There have been countless times when I spoke harshly, sent a nasty email, or made a bad decision that caused irreparable damage. Compounding the problem, there never seemed to be a shortage of internal and external voices telling me that my mistake couldn't be fixed and that I ruined the holiday, situation, or relationship forever. As the story of Adam and Eve reveals, however, that is a flat-out lie. Any thoughts that God can't fix my mistakes are rooted in pride. No matter how badly any of us messes up, we're not powerful enough to thwart the Lord's ability to bring good out of our mistakes.

Instead of trying to anticipate how the Lord will fix our mistakes, we should take comfort in the saga of Adam and Eve. No matter what you've done and how much damage it caused, your situation pales in comparison. If God can bring good out of the mess they caused, he can do the same in your life. All that's needed is your cooperation and patience. It might not be pretty and you might have to accept some of the lingering fallout, but something positive can come out of it.

PRAYER

Dear God, the story of Adam and Eve really says a lot about you. Even though they didn't apologize for their disobedience, you were merciful and stepped in to correct the damage they caused. Please come into my life and repair any damage caused by my bad choices. Grant me the humility necessary to accept responsibility and take corrective action if needed. I ask this in Jesus's name. Amen.

DISCUSSION QUESTIONS

1. Why do you think it was so difficult for Eve to obey God's command? When have you experienced the same tempting feelings that led her to eat of the fruit?

2. What role does Adam play in Eve's disobedience? (Hint: Read Genesis 3:1–6 carefully. If Eve was immediately able to share the fruit with Adam, what can you conclude about his proximity during her encounter with the serpent?)

3. Think of a situation when you messed up in a big way. How did you feel? What bothered you the most? Does

the story of Adam and Eve change the way you look at this situation?

Chapter 3

WHEN GOD IS LATE (LAZARUS)

John 11:1-47

Being all-powerful and all-knowing makes it impossible for God to make a mistake. But there are times when it just doesn't seem as if he made the best decision. And because we know he has total control, it's easy to blame God when things don't work out the way we like.

I have lived through this scenario many times, with the most memorable being my father's cancer diagnosis in 2002. Even though the prognosis wasn't good, I prayed that God would perform a miraculous healing. In my mind, it seemed to be the appropriate solution. My mother was in the early stages of dementia and depended on my dad for many things. Restoring my father to good health made sense to me, but apparently not to God. When my father died one month after his initial diagnosis, it was easy to point the finger at God. There was only one person who could have spared my dad's life—and he chose not to. Why *shouldn't* I blame God?

THE FACTS

In chapter 11 of John's gospel, we're introduced to Lazarus of Bethany, the brother of Martha and Mary. We learn that he was a close friend of Jesus and that he was ill. As a result, the sisters sent word to Jesus, who responded with what seemed to be comforting news: "This illness is not unto death; it is for the glory of God, so that the Son of God may be glorified by means of it" (Jn 11:4).

After speaking those words, Jesus did something that seems odd. Instead of rushing to the bedside of his sick friend, he stayed two days longer "in the place where he was" (Jn 11:6). When Jesus decided it was time to travel to Judea to "wake up" Lazarus, he made a mind-boggling comment to his disciples. Having just told them that this sickness was "not unto death," he explains that Lazarus is, in fact, dead.

By the time Jesus arrived in Bethany, Lazarus had been in the tomb for four days. Hearing that Jesus was near, Martha left the house to meet him. Her words were direct and to the point: "Lord, if you had been here, my brother would not have died" (Jn 11:21). Her words may have conveyed a sense of finality and regret, but she went on to say something that seemed to indicate that she wasn't looking at this as a done deal. Martha expressed her belief that "even now" the Father would grant whatever Jesus asked of him (Jn 11:22). He replied by stating that Lazarus would rise again.

Then Martha summoned Mary, indicating that Jesus wished to see her. Mary's words to Jesus were practically identical to Martha's, minus the hopefulness. It was solely an "if only you had been here" message. When Mary and the other friends of Jesus began to weep, Jesus was deeply moved and joined them in weeping. He then asked to see where Lazarus was buried and went to the tomb.

After Jesus ordered the stone to be removed, Martha seemed to waver and pointed out just how much a stench a four-day-old corpse would have. Standing firm, Jesus addressed her with a reminder: "Did I not tell you that if you would believe you would see the glory of God?" (Jn 11:40).

Once the stone was removed, Jesus offered a prayer to his Father and then ordered Lazarus to "come out" (Jn 11:43). He did just that. As a result, many of the Jews believed in the power of Jesus.

A CLOSER LOOK

The story of Lazarus is so familiar that it's easy to overlook many of the supporting details. Yes, Jesus miraculously raised his friend from the dead, but we don't want to gloss over the specifics. In my opinion, that's where an extremely far-fetched and distant event becomes real and very personal.

Jesus's first words upon hearing of his friend's illness are very comforting: "This illness is not unto death." If I was present and heard those words, I would almost certainly conclude that Lazarus would recover from his illness. After looking at how the events played out, however, it's hard to reconcile what Jesus said with the fact that Lazarus died. Didn't he say that this illness wouldn't end in death?

In reality, there's nothing contradictory about his words. Jesus never stated that Lazarus wouldn't die. What he said was that the sickness wouldn't *end* in death and that it would glorify God. Jesus often has a totally different perspective than we do. We may view death as something final, but Jesus sees it as a starting point.

Did you find it odd that Jesus responded to the news of Lazarus's illness by staying put for two more days? It almost seems that he was purposely waiting for his friend to die. I believe that's exactly what he was doing. But why would he let that happen, especially when Martha and Mary asked for his intervention?

My guess is that he wanted to strengthen their faith. Judging by their comments when Jesus arrived on the scene ("Lord, if you had been here, my brother would not have died"), Martha and Mary believed in his power to heal Lazarus. But did they believe that he could raise someone from the dead? It sure didn't sound like it. By the end of the story, however, they would believe, and so would all those who witnessed the miracle. A miraculous healing would have been amazing, but raising a corpse from the dead takes it to a whole different level.

Ultimately, the sisters of Lazarus asked Jesus for something good, but Jesus had something even better in mind for them. In order to give them what they needed, however, he first had to allow them to experience some suffering. You can't experience the glorious joy of a resurrection without first grieving over a death. Their grief may have been temporary, but it was very real.

Speaking of grief, there's one last point that must be made about this story. It's understandable that the relatives of Lazarus were distraught, but why did Jesus weep? It's hard to imagine that he didn't know what he was about to do. Why would he cry when he was about to perform a miracle and restore his friend to life? A close look at the details of the story gives us a clue: "When Jesus saw her weeping, and the Jews who came with her also weeping, he was deeply moved in spirit and troubled" (Jn 11:33).

He may have known what was about to happen, but nobody else did. At that moment in time, his compassion for those who grieved the loss of their loved one was so strong that it moved him to tears. That's a powerful insight into how Jesus cares for us when we grieve. The fact that he can see the bigger picture doesn't stop him from grieving with us when we can't.

WHY IT MATTERS

This is a great story with a great ending, but as is typical for most of the stories in this book, it's difficult to see the good while the plot is still unfolding. Ultimately, what we can learn from the saga of Lazarus is that when God answers our prayers with a no, it's only because he has something even better in mind. But it's hard to see and celebrate the "something better" when we're overwhelmed with pain and sorrow. Once Lazarus walked out of the tomb, I'd be willing to bet that nobody complained that Jesus was late and let him die. Before the miracle took place, however, it was a totally different story.

Was it God's fault that my father died when I prayed for him to be healed? I certainly felt like it was. He could have miraculously healed my dad by driving out the cancer, but he didn't. As the days passed, however, my outlook began to change. Even though my dad's death made it more difficult to handle my mother's deteriorating mental state, I stopped feeling like it was God's fault and began to view it as God's intervention. Although I didn't pray for my father to die, he was no longer suffering from the pain caused by the cancer. His inability to taste his favorite foods (caused by the chemo) was no longer an issue. My father no longer had to use a walker to strengthen the legs that were weakened by the cancer. In addition, my sister and I were now able to get my mother the long-term care that she needed. Even though I still missed my dad, God's fault gradually became God's blessing.

As we conclude our look at the story of Lazarus, I want to leave you with a final thought. God can bring good out of all things, but that process may still involve suffering. Furthermore, we're not entirely wrong to attribute that suffering to his actions or lack thereof. Let's not forget that Jesus allowed Lazarus to die. He did it in order to perform a greater miracle, but he still allowed it to happen. And his death, albeit temporary, caused tremendous suffering for Martha, Mary, and many others. Jesus himself reacted to that suffering. It caused him to cry.

The death of Lazarus was an interim step on the way to a greater good, but the mourners didn't see it that way. If the Lord is allowing you to experience something similar, it's also because a greater good lies ahead. You may not see it now. In fact, you may not see or understand it in this life. But just as Jesus wept with the family of Lazarus, he weeps with you too. He may allow you to be in a situation that causes you to suffer, but he'll never allow you to go through it alone.

PRAYER

Dear Jesus, I totally get where Martha and Mary were coming from when they questioned your actions. I don't understand why you didn't answer my prayer. It's not like I was asking for something bad. What could possibly have been wrong with what I wanted? Even though I'm struggling to see the good in what you did, however, that's not my immediate problem. Right now, I need you to weep with me and bring me some comfort. I'm really suffering right now. Please don't leave me. Amen.

DISCUSSION QUESTIONS

1. Jesus could have simply healed Lazarus of his illness, as he did with many others, but it was actually better to let him die first. What are the situations in your life that you are waiting for Jesus to fix? If he does not help in the way you hope, what greater good might be standing on the other side of your pain and sorrow?

2. Do you blame God for something that happened in your past or something you're going through now? Compose a brief prayer telling him exactly how you feel.

3. What do the comments of Martha and Mary tell us about the strength and weakness of their faith? What lesson(s) can you learn from them?

Chapter 4

WHEN OTHERS MESS UP (JOSEPH)

Genesis 37-50

When I was in elementary school in Philadelphia, it was common practice for the eighth graders to take a big field trip at the end of the year. Instead of the typical trip to the zoo, a park, or a local museum, those in the eighth grade usually went to New York City or Washington, DC. It was definitely a bigger deal than the trips taken by the lower grades.

At some point in my eighth-grade year, we were informed that our field trip was being canceled due to bad behavior. As a quiet student who was scared to death of getting into trouble, I thought that this punishment was totally unjustified. I didn't do anything wrong. Why should I suffer the consequences for the bad behavior of others? It was not fair!

I was learning the difficult lesson that suffering the consequences caused by someone else's behavior is part of life.

Joseph, one of the twelve sons of Jacob, knew firsthand what it's like to suffer because of someone else's actions. His story illustrates the fact that, even though God doesn't will evil, God can use it to bring about a greater good. It's a lesson that can definitely soften the blow brought about by the unfairness of life.

THE FACTS

The Bible first introduces us to Joseph as a seventeen-year-old who was tending sheep. Joseph was hated by his brothers because they knew Jacob loved him most. One day, Joseph shared with his brothers a dream where he saw them bowing down to him. Their hatred for him grew stronger, and they sold him to a caravan of Ishmaelites bound for Egypt. The brothers covered their tracks by dipping Joseph's robe in the blood of a slaughtered goat and presenting it to their father, who concluded that Joseph was devoured by a wild animal.

Once in Egypt, Joseph was purchased by one of Pharoah's officials named Potiphar. Because "the LORD was with Joseph" (Gn 39:2), however, he was able to prosper and succeed in everything he did. Eventually, Joseph was put in charge of Potiphar's household and became his attendant. Ultimately, the young man was given responsibility over all of his master's possessions. Everything was going well for Joseph until he rejected the sexual advances of Potiphar's wife. In her anger, she convinced her

When Others Mess Up (Joseph)

husband that it was Joseph who was seducing her. As a result, Joseph was placed in prison.

Again, however, the Lord looked with favor on Joseph, and he was placed in charge of the other prisoners. Just as before, he was successful in everything he did. With God's assistance, Joseph was able to successfully interpret Pharoah's dream (which predicted seven years of abundance followed by seven years of famine) and was placed in charge of all of Egypt. Knowing that a famine was on the way, Joseph took advantage of the seven years of abundance by ordering the stockpiling of all the grain that was harvested.

After seven years, the famine occurred just as predicted, but Egypt had an abundance of stored-up grain. Pharoah sent the Egyptians to Joseph to buy the grain needed to survive. When the famine spread to the entire world, Jacob sent ten of his sons to buy grain in Egypt, not knowing that Joseph was alive and in charge of the grain supply.

When Joseph's brothers arrived, they didn't recognize him—but he recognized them. After multiple encounters, Joseph let them in on the secret and they were understandably stunned. He urged them to have no fear and not to be angry with themselves, because "God sent me before you to preserve life" (Gn 45:5).

Eventually, Jacob was brought to Egypt and reunited with Joseph. When Jacob died, his sons worried that Joseph would hold a grudge against them and attempt to seek revenge for how they treated him. Begging for forgiveness, the brothers threw themselves at Joseph's feet and pleaded for leniency. Joseph responded by saying, "Fear not, for am I in the place of God? As for you, you meant evil against me; but God meant it for good, to bring it about that many people should be kept alive, as they are today. So do not fear; I will provide for you and your little ones" (Gn 50:19–21).

This story offers a powerful example of God bringing good out of evil. Even though Joseph's brothers clearly intended evil, God used their actions to provide for the needs of his children.

A CLOSER LOOK

The story of Joseph reminds us that God's will is unstoppable. No matter how many terrible things happened to Joseph, God always managed to bring him to a better place. What strikes me most about the story of Joseph, however, is that his victory started with an evil act that looked like the ultimate example of defeat. Even though it would be a bumpy ride and looked pretty ugly at times, God would eventually lead Joseph to a very good place.

God did not will for Joseph to be sold into slavery. The evil action taken by the brothers was their choice alone. It was born out of hatred, mainly because they were envious of Joseph's highly favored status with Jacob. Joseph didn't help himself by bragging about those dreams, but there's still no way he deserved what happened to him.

Here's the amazing thing about how God operates: he wasn't fazed in the least by what happened to Joseph. As he often does, he took the broken pieces caused by the brothers' devious plot and worked with them to create something new and life-giving. He had a plan for Joseph, and no amount of evil was going to get in the way.

As bad as it was, getting sold to the Ishmaelites wasn't the only unfair event that Joseph would experience. When he tried to do the right thing and reject the advances of Potiphar's wife, Joseph ended up in prison for several years—hardly the type of treatment we would expect for someone favored by God, but that's what happened.

Finally, because of his God-given gift to interpret dreams, Joseph found favor in the eyes of Pharaoh and ended up as his second-in-command. After many years of suffering and being subject to "unfair" circumstances, Joseph seemed to be in the clear. The story was far from over, however. Even though things were looking good in Joseph's life, God had plans to bless many other people. By the time this story ends, many more benefited from God's providence, including those who perpetrated the evil in the first place!

No doubt about it, there are plenty of ugly details contained in this story. There's also a lot of unfairness. It wasn't Joseph's fault that Jacob loved him best. It wasn't fair that his brothers sold him into slavery. It wasn't fair that he ended up in prison when he was trying to do the right thing. Through it all, however, God helped Joseph and others by making good out of evil.

Here's what I like best about the story of Joseph. If we zoom out and gloss over all of the sordid details, we have a story of God providing for his children in the midst of a famine. It wasn't God's will that Joseph's brothers sold him to the Ishmaelites, but by allowing it to happen, he ensured that Joseph was in the right place at the right time. It took many years to play out and involved suffering for many people, but the end result is undeniable: God provides. We may not understand his methods and may not like his timetable, but the Creator takes care of his creatures.

WHY IT MATTERS

Dealing with the consequences caused by the actions of others is a fact of life. It may be something small like being forced to spend extra time in the checkout line because of the incompetence of the cashier, or it could involve the bigger issue of having to pick up the slack for a coworker who is negligent in performing their duties. Sometimes it involves a major catastrophe, such as marital infidelity or even abuse, violence, or murder.

The story of Joseph enables us to move forward with hope, knowing that God can bring good out of the careless, malicious, or even criminal actions of others. Yes, we may have to suffer unpleasant consequences for a while, but we can have faith that things are still ordered for our good. Unfortunately, the longer our suffering continues, the easier it is to lose hope. That's why the story of Joseph is so important. It teaches us that God's plan for our lives cannot be stopped by the mistakes or evil actions of others. It may take time and it may get ugly, but the Lord's hands aren't tied when one of his creatures messes up.

For me, that's good news. No matter how badly someone damages my life by their actions, God's will for my life cannot be thwarted. I still have to get past the fact that my plans may come to a screeching halt or that I'll have to suffer, but I can take comfort in knowing that God can still bring good out of it. It may not always be the good I want, but it's the good that God wants for me.

In addition to learning about God's providence in times of famine, Joseph and his brothers were taught a lesson about forgiveness and second chances. Joseph may have also learned about patience and trust during his ordeal.

As we bring this chapter to a close, I want to make sure that you don't think I'm suggesting that we just "grin and bear it" while waiting for God to bring good out of our misery. Once we surrender to God's will, the fact that life isn't fair becomes a much smaller issue. Accepting the fact that life isn't fair ultimately comes down to surrendering to God's will. Once again, God doesn't will evil, but he permits it because he can use it for good. Turning our lives over to God puts us in a position to receive his peace. Even though we may have to suffer at times, we can find peace by accepting the uncontrollable circumstances of life. God wants us to be at peace in this life and live with him forever in heaven in the next life. The actions of others, no matter how damaging or malicious, cannot stop either of those two things from happening. Just ask Joseph.

PRAYER

Dear Holy Spirit, I have a difficult time understanding why I have to suffer because of the actions of others. It's even more painful when the actions are malicious and designed to hurt me. Because you possess infinite wisdom and can see the big picture, please help me to understand.

And even if I can't fully comprehend God's reasoning, help me at least to accept that he has a plan and that it will work out for the best. Amen.

DISCUSSION QUESTIONS

1. Have you ever suffered major consequences from the actions of another? How did it make you feel? What did you learn from that experience?

2. Try to put yourself in the place of Joseph as he's being transported to Egypt, or when he's sitting in a jail cell. What are you thinking about your future and about your brothers?

3. What can you learn about God and the way he operates from the story of Joseph? How can this lesson help you going forward?

Chapter 5

WHEN BAD STUFF HAPPENS (RUTH AND NAOMI)

Ruth 1-4

In the past few chapters, we've looked at how God can bring good out of situations when someone is at fault. Although there's always the challenge to start finger-pointing or to ponder, "What if?," having a perpetrator gives us a clean starting point. Justified or not, we can at least begin our quest for God's goodness by recognizing the fact that someone caused the problem.

What about the cases where nobody is at fault? When our starting point is a flood, earthquake, tornado, fire, or something that "just happens," it can be difficult to begin our journey to find the good. If we're not careful, we can falsely convince ourselves that God doesn't care about the bad things in life that "just happen." But this is totally untrue. He really does care. Fortunately, the Bible gives us a story of how God can bring good out of a case like this.

The book of Ruth begins with the news of a difficult situation that wasn't anyone's fault: a famine. This crisis forced a man named Elimelech to travel to the hostile land of Moab, thus beginning a chain of events that would display the goodness and power of God. Just as in the story of Joseph, a famine is involved, but there's a big difference. Unlike the story of Joseph and his brothers, which begins with an evil action that is definitely someone's fault, the story of Ruth commences with a famine that is technically nobody's fault. In both cases, however, the end result is the same. It took him a while and there were many twists and turns, but God brought good out of both situations.

THE FACTS

As the book of Ruth opens, we learn that Elimelech responded to an ongoing famine in Bethlehem by taking his wife, Naomi, and two sons to the land of Moab. In the first few verses of the book, we are informed of Elimelech's death and the marriage of his sons to Moabite women, Ruth and Orpah. Verse five delivers the bad news that the two sons died after ten years, leaving Naomi, Ruth, and Orpah alone without any means of support.

Learning that the famine in Judah had come to an end and having no reason to remain in Moab, Naomi made the decision to return home. Although she started on the journey with her two daughters-in-law, Naomi reconsidered and urged the women to remain in Moab so they could find new husbands. Orpah kissed her mother-in-law goodbye and obeyed, but Ruth refused to leave

Naomi's side. When the two women arrived in Bethlehem, Naomi was so frustrated that she changed her own name to Mara, which means "bitter." She did this because of her belief that the Lord had treated her bitterly.

Because they arrived in town at the beginning of the barley harvest and needed some way to provide for themselves, Ruth went into the field to pick up any leftover grain that remained on the ground. While working in the field, she met a successful man named Boaz. Impressed with the kindness that Ruth had displayed to Naomi, Boaz ensured that the young woman would be permitted to continue collecting the scraps of grain without being disturbed by the other workers.

Boaz and Ruth went on to get married, and Naomi now had someone to provide for her needs. The couple had a son they named Obed, who would become the father of Jesse, the father of King David.

A CLOSER LOOK

While this story definitely has a happy ending, it needs to be read all the way through before the good news becomes apparent. If you stopped reading after the fifth verse, this whole situation looks like a total disaster. Naomi is stuck in a foreign land with no husband and no sons to support her. And the whole mess started with a famine. If it wasn't for the shortage of food, Naomi would have had no reason to leave her homeland in the first place. Instead, she found herself abandoned in a hostile land in a very bad situation. How does Naomi feel about what has happened to her? When she and Ruth arrived back home in Bethlehem, she told her neighbors, "Do not call me Na'omi, call me Mara, for the Almighty has dealt very bitterly with me. I went away full, and the Lord has brought me back empty. Why call me Na'omi, when the LORD has afflicted me and the Almighty has brought calamity upon me?" (Ru 1:20–21).

Well, that's interesting. Naomi isn't blaming the famine for her misfortune—she's blaming *God*. It is not revealed until later in the story (Ru 4:3), but her husband still owned property in Bethlehem. If it wasn't for the disruption caused by the famine, she could have lived on this land or possibly sold it for a profit.

This brings us to a key point in the story and in this book. Could it have been possible that Naomi was right and all of this, including the famine, was actually God's doing? By skipping ahead in the story and reading between the lines a bit, I believe it's possible to answer that question. In order to do so, however, it will be necessary for us to confront a question that we spend a lot of time trying to avoid: Is God responsible for famines, fires, earthquakes, and other natural disasters—or do they "just happen"?

Because famines are typically caused by lack of rainfall, let's begin with a basic question: Does God produce or withhold rain? While there are many Bible verses that support the position that he is indeed the one who makes

When Bad Stuff Happens (Ruth and Naomi)

it rain, my favorite example occurs on the Sea of Galilee when Jesus calmed a violent storm with the simple command, "Peace! Be still!" (Mk 4:39). If the Lord can command the storm to cease, what would prevent him from doing the same with the rain?

If God controls the rain, and I believe that is indeed the case, then we are now forced to deal with the obvious question as we look at the story of Naomi and her family: Why would an all-loving God allow a destructive famine to take place, especially when it would cause hunger, turmoil, and death for his children?

Quite possibly, as the story of Naomi and Ruth suggests, he did it to guide them down a path that would produce even greater good. It's a path that they wouldn't have ordinarily traveled without some sort of intervention.

Let's examine the facts. Because there was no food in the land, Naomi and her family traveled to Moab. While there, Ruth became her daughter-in-law. When God ended the famine, Ruth and Naomi returned to Bethlehem, where Ruth met and married Boaz and they had a son named Obed. All of this goodness came out of a famine that appeared to be nobody's fault.

In case we need some additional evidence to support the goodness that came out of this situation, Naomi's friends from Bethlehem connected the dots: "Then the women said to Na'omi, 'Blessed be the LORD, who has not left you this day without next of kin; and may his name be renowned in Israel! He shall be to you a restorer of life and a nourisher of your old age; for your daughter-in-law who loves you, who is more to you than seven sons, has borne him'" (Ru 4:14–15).

As we prepare to leave this story, I'd like you to consider some additional goodness that not only benefited Naomi, but can benefit you as well. The book of Ruth is not the last time Ruth, Boaz, and Obed are mentioned in the Bible. Their names are also recorded in Matthew's genealogy of Jesus Christ: "Abraham was the father of Isaac, and Isaac the father of Jacob . . . and Salmon the father of Boaz by Rahab, and Boaz the father of Obed by Ruth, and Obed the father of Jesse, and Jesse the father of David the king" (Mt 1:2, 5–6). Jesus the Messiah is descended from Obed, who was born to a husband and wife who met because God chose to stop and start the rain. Nobody is to blame for the weather? I'm not so sure.

WHY IT MATTERS

Now that we've examined the story of Ruth and Naomi, let's look at why it matters to us. Almost every day, we hear of some sort of natural disaster that causes death and destruction. As an almost-necessary defense mechanism, we respond by attributing these events to happenstance. In other words, these destructive occurrences are part of nature and are nobody's fault. God's involvement in them is deemphasized or denied in order to avoid making the connection that he is the cause of the associated misery and suffering, which is true. God does not want us to experience the evil of suffering, and he does not impose this suffering upon us.

But the danger in disassociating God from these violent acts of nature is that we relegate him to the position of being a helpless or uninterested bystander. The Lord is not a distant and uncaring supreme being. Not only is that claim depressing, but it's totally inaccurate.

In order to recognize that God can help us with the painful struggles of life, we must first acknowledge his omnipotence. If he can't even control the weather, why should I believe that he can cure my illness or help me with my finances? It's critical to know that God loves me unconditionally, but it's also important to know that he has power over all those things that I can't control.

Deism is a philosophy that originated in the seventeenth century. Its core belief centers on a supreme being who created the universe but does not intervene in it. While this way of thinking can make it easier to reconcile a loving God with the devastation caused by natural disasters, it is completely at odds with Christianity. The "hands-off" supreme being recognized by deists would never consider entering our world by taking on a human nature.

Because God is both all-powerful and all-loving, he is able to use the circumstances of life in a way that is most beneficial to his children. That means that he is able to allow a flood or earthquake to take place and use it to help us in some way. It can motivate us to exercise charity toward those whose lives were affected by the disaster, it can help us to understand the temporary nature of this life, and it can give us the opportunity to turn to him in our hour of need and let him help us. As in the case of Naomi and her family, it can even give God a chance to send us a Savior.

PRAYER

Dear Father, when I look at natural disasters, it's easiest to view them as being nobody's fault. If I admit that you have power over them, I have to go down the uncomfortable path of wondering why you would allow so many innocent people to suffer or die. Ignoring your power over these events, however, makes me wonder if you really are all-powerful. I don't have to understand why you let these events happen, but I do need to trust that you know what you're doing. Please increase my confidence in you, even when I don't understand your actions. I ask this in the name of Jesus. Amen.

DISCUSSION QUESTIONS

1. What benefits are there to not being able to understand everything that God does? What would it say about him if you could understand all of his actions?

2. Think of a natural disaster, recent or otherwise, and come up with a list of potential benefits that could have come from it. Could those same benefits have come about if the disaster never happened?

3. Some of the good that came from the story of Naomi and Ruth wasn't apparent until all of the parties were deceased. What does that teach you about God's timetable for bringing good out of a bad situation?

Chapter 6

WHEN YOUR DREAM FALLS APART (DISCIPLES ON THE ROAD TO EMMAUS)

Luke 24:13-49

I first met Lou when I was working as a software developer. He was several years older than I was, but we became good friends. Like me, Lou struggled greatly with work-related anxiety. We would often commiserate with one another about everything that was wrong in the workplace. He would often speak about how much he looked forward to retirement. A lifelong bachelor, Lou had many hobbies, including skiing and fishing. He absolutely valued his time away from the office, as it gave him some much-needed peace.

One day, Lou informed me that he had made the decision to retire. Even though he hadn't yet reached retirement age, he had put away enough savings and investments to get by. He was very excited and looked forward to obtaining the peace that had eluded him for so many years. I would certainly miss having Lou around, but I was happy for him.

Shortly after he retired, Lou was diagnosed with an aggressive form of cancer. His retirement dreams were shattered and his life was turned upside down. Instead of spending his days fishing and skiing, he spent most of his time in the hospital. He struggled to cope, as this wasn't the way "it was supposed to be."

The two travelers on the road to Emmaus knew what it was like to have their dreams fall apart as well. Hoping that Jesus was going to redeem Israel, they struggled to make sense of his Crucifixion. Their hope for the future died with Jesus on the Cross. What would they do now that their Messiah was dead? Just like Lou, they struggled to put together the pieces. This wasn't the way it was supposed to be.

THE FACTS

On the day that Jesus rose from the dead, two individuals were traveling on the road to a village named Emmaus, which is located seven miles from Jerusalem. The Gospel of Luke tells us that one of them is named Cleopas, but the other is not named. As they walked, they talked with each other about the events of the past few days.

Jesus himself joined them on the journey, but they didn't recognize him. When he asked what they were

When Your Dream Falls Apart (Disciples on the Road to Emmaus)

discussing, the two stopped and looked sad. Cleopas responded with a question of his own, asking Jesus if he was the only visitor to Jerusalem who didn't know what just happened. Playing along, Jesus asked for more information. Cleopas responded, "Concerning Jesus of Nazareth, who was a prophet mighty in deed and word before God and all the people, and how our chief priests and rulers delivered him up to be condemned to death, and crucified him. But we had hoped that he was the one to redeem Israel. Yes, and besides all this, it is now the third day since this happened" (Lk 24:19–21). Cleopas went on to tell their still-unrecognized traveling companion that some women reported that the tomb was empty and that they had seen a vision of angels, who said that Jesus had risen from the dead.

At that point, Jesus chided the two travelers for failing to believe what the prophets had spoken about the Messiah. He then went on to give them a scripture refresher course, pointing out all of the prophecies concerning the Messiah's life, death, and resurrection. Still not recognizing him, they invited Jesus to stay with them, as it was getting late. Joining them for a meal, Jesus took bread, blessed it, broke it, and gave it to them. Suddenly, their eyes were opened and they recognized him. With that, Jesus vanished and they were left wondering what had just happened.

They returned to Jerusalem and shared the news that they had met Jesus with the apostles, who confirmed the news by reporting that the risen Lord had also appeared to Simon. As they continued to discuss what just took place, Jesus appeared and stood among them. Questioning their lack of peace, Jesus opened their minds to understand the scriptures and told them to remain in Jerusalem until they received the power of the Holy Spirit.

A CLOSER LOOK

On the day that Jesus rose from the dead, we read of two travelers journeying to a village named Emmaus. In his gospel narrative, Luke writes that they were discussing "these things that had happened" (Lk 24:14). The specifics of their conversation are not revealed until Jesus shows up (unrecognized) and asks them what they were discussing. Even before they answer him, however, we have a good idea of what they were thinking when we learn that they "stood still, looking sad" (Lk 24:17).

Fortunately for us, Jesus's question allows the travelers to elaborate on the reason for their sadness. They were hoping that Jesus was going to be the one to redeem Israel, but their dream fell apart three days earlier when he was condemned to death and crucified. They explain that his body was missing and that some women were informed by angels that Jesus was alive.

Before we consider how these individuals could have missed the point of what just happened and who they were conversing with, let's look at where they were mentally. Their dreams were shattered and they were

When Your Dream Falls Apart (Disciples on the Road to Emmaus)

distraught. In their minds, this wasn't the way it was supposed to be.

First, I think we need to cut Cleopas and his companion some slack. They were not the only ones who looked at the empty tomb and failed to recognize that something great had just happened. Some of Jesus's closest friends, such as Mary Magdalene and several of the apostles, missed the point too. Even though Jesus clearly stated that he would be put to death and rise on the third day, his followers could have been in denial, preoccupied with other matters, or maybe just incapable of understanding. The brutality of the Crucifixion coupled with the emptiness of the tomb may just have been too much for them.

Part of the problem could also have been caused by the fact that, like so many others, these two were looking for a messiah who would come in power and put an end to the oppression of the Roman regime. Of course, that's never what the scriptures promised, but it's still what they expected. The idea of a king who would reign from a cross over a kingdom that's not of this world is not easy to accept. Heck, I still struggle with this reality almost every day when I look at the craziness taking place around me. If it's a difficult concept to grasp now, it had to be a whole lot tougher then when they lacked the benefit of perspective. Their dreams were based on what they thought would happen. No matter what they were taught beforehand, watching the crucifixion, death, and burial of their king had to have taken its toll on them.

Here's what I like about the way Jesus handled this situation: he was determined to come to the assistance of the two companions whose dreams had been shattered. Even though they should have known better, he didn't hold it against them. He went looking for them and stayed with them until they realized that he was alive. Yes, they would have to rethink their initial dreams, but the reality of a risen Savior would enable them to dream even bigger dreams.

Ultimately, it was Jesus's unpacking the scriptures and breaking bread that turned their sadness into joy. It's difficult to look at his actions and not associate them with what we experience at Mass. Isn't it comforting to know that we too can experience what the two travelers experienced on the road to Emmaus? Finding peace in the midst of broken dreams begins with the knowledge that Jesus Christ is alive and is walking beside us.

WHY IT MATTERS

The story of the two travelers on the road to Emmaus is essentially a story of individuals whose dreams fell apart. They expected events to play out a certain way and they did not. More importantly, it's a story about a dream that is too small. Even though what they desired was a good thing, God wanted them to have something even better. Freedom from Roman occupation through an earthly king would not have been a bad thing for them, but eternal life in heaven and the ability to experience peace even in the

When Your Dream Falls Apart (Disciples on the Road to Emmaus)

midst of serious troubles is much greater. In fact, what the Lord ended up giving them is something so supremely good that they wouldn't have even thought to dream of it. That's why they settled for something that their minds *could* grasp.

We spend a lot of time planning how things should work out in order to bring us happiness, and we often get very specific in our expectations. We are convinced that if we only made more money, became famous, had a bigger house, had more opportunities, found a new job, or retired from work altogether—then we would be happy. We often get so locked into our dreams that we don't consider that something else could make us just as happy, or even happier. As a result, when these specific dreams don't pan out, we often become discouraged or even distraught. We conclude that our chance for happiness vanished with our dreams. That is simply not true.

I can't even begin to count how many times I have been so locked into a specific outcome that I was devastated when it didn't turn out. My attitude could even be seen in my prayers as I told the Lord that this relationship, job, promotion, speaking engagement, or radio show was what I needed to be happy. As I look back now, even though I'm still not totally free from this way of thinking, I'm thankful that he didn't always listen to me. Many of those "guaranteed happiness" outcomes would have been disastrous had they occurred. It's a difficult lesson to learn, but our carefully constructed dreams aren't always good for us. Fortunately, we have a heavenly Father who knows what is good for us.

I never finished telling you about my friend Lou. In addition to being burdened by the pressure of the job, Lou was terrified of cancer and the needles involved in healthcare. When he would go each year for his annual checkup, he dreaded the inevitable blood test and the always-possible cancer diagnosis. So I can't tell you how surprised I was when I went to visit him in the hospital and found him in good spirits, despite having several needles in his arms and battling cancer. We chatted about our faith and had a good laugh about the needles. I saw a new Lou in that moment. Despite the uncertainty and pain, he seemed to be at peace. He died a few months later—"with a smile on his face," according to his sister. Lou had thought that a life free from the pressures of work and filled with his favorite hobbies would bring him peace, but the Lord knew better. Lou found his peace through a cancer diagnosis and by walking beside Jesus Christ. Lou's dreams may have crumbled, but he ended up with much more happiness than he ever thought possible.

PRAYER

Dear Jesus, thank you for walking beside me. As you know, I'm struggling to find happiness after my dreams fell apart. I may not feel it right now, but I know you can "fix" me. Help me to be patient if your "fixing" doesn't happen as fast as I'd like. Please make yourself known to me, just as you did with the travelers on the road to Emmaus. I think I know why only Cleopas is named in Luke's gospel account. That other disciple struggling to find peace in the midst of broken dreams is me. Help me, Lord. Amen.

DISCUSSION QUESTIONS

1. Why do you think the travelers didn't instantly recognize Jesus when they encountered him? Have you had an experience of suffering that has blinded you to a person or situation that should have been obvious?

2. Do you think it's possible that Jesus knew what the two travelers were discussing? If so, why would he ask them about it? How does this dialogue benefit the reader of the story? How did it benefit the travelers?

3. What steps have you taken to regain your peace after your dreams fell apart in the past? How long did it take to recover?

Chapter 7

WHEN YOU'VE BEEN USED, REJECTED, OR ABANDONED (HAGAR)

Genesis 16:1-15; 21:8-21

I would venture to guess that most of us have suffered the indignity of being used by another person at one time or another. Worse is being used and subsequently rejected when we are no longer deemed useful. Worst of all, however, is to be used, rejected, and then totally abandoned. All of a sudden, an emotionally painful situation now becomes dangerous or even life-threatening. That worst-case scenario is exactly what happened to a woman named Hagar. It's a story that warrants a closer look.

Hagar was the maid (more accurately, slave) of Abraham's wife Sarah, and she found herself in the middle of a crazy plan designed to force God to act. It was not a good plan, but, because of her role, Hagar didn't have much of a say in the matter. Nonetheless, she suffered greatly because of the selfishness of Sarah and Abraham. The good news is that there is a happy ending. Seeing her plight, the Lord intervened and brought good out of an ugly situation. It's a story that offers comfort to anyone who has ever felt used, rejected, or even abandoned.

THE FACTS

Abraham's wife Sarah was tired of waiting for God to deliver on his promise of sending them a child, so she came up with a plan to help him along. This is the plan, in her own words, as she relayed it to Abraham: "Behold now, the LORD has prevented me from bearing children; go in to my maid; it may be that I shall obtain children by her" (Gn 16:2).

As far-fetched and wrong as the idea sounds, Abraham went along with it. Sarah gave Hagar to her husband as a wife, and she conceived a child. Despite the fact that it was all Sarah's idea, she now looked at Hagar with contempt. Abraham gave Sarah permission to deal with her maid as she wished. The harsh treatment that followed caused Hagar to flee from her mistress.

Finding her in the wilderness by the water, the angel of the Lord urged Hagar to return to Sarah and submit to her. The angel instructed her to name her child Ishmael, which means "God hears." Realizing that God saw the way she was treated, Hagar called him "a God of seeing" (Gn 16:13; *El-Roi*, in Hebrew).

Abraham was eighty-six when the child was born, and he obeyed the Lord by naming the child Ishmael as he was instructed. Fourteen years later, Abraham and Sarah had a son of their own and named him Isaac. One day, after the child grew older, Sarah saw Isaac playing with Ishmael, and she was not pleased. Going to Abraham, she instructed her husband to send Hagar and Ishmael away. Surprisingly, God told Abraham to obey his wife. Waking up early, he packed some food for them and sent the mother and son on their way. Hagar and Ishmael ended up wandering in the wilderness.

When their water was gone, Hagar pleaded for her child's life as he cried out. Hearing his cries, the Lord responded by promising to make him a great nation. Suddenly, Hagar's eyes were opened and she saw a well of water. Drawing some water from the well, she gave her son a drink. The story draws to a close as follows: "And God was with the lad, and he grew up; he lived in the wilderness, and became an expert with the bow. He lived in the wilderness of Paran; and his mother took a wife for him from the land of Egypt" (Gn 21:20–21).

God cares about all of his children, especially those who are helpless. Everyone else may have rejected Hagar and Ishmael, but God didn't forget them. When Ishmael cried for lack of water, the Lord heard his cries and provided the well. As a result, the child survived, got married, and was in a position to provide for his helpless mother.

A CLOSER LOOK

There is so much going on in the story of Abraham and Sarah that the subplot featuring Hagar and Ishmael can easily get glossed over. The entire saga is definitely worth a read (we'll take a look at another incident in the life of Abraham later), but the goal of this chapter is to concentrate on Hagar. She was used, rejected, and abandoned, but God took care of her.

Because she was basically a slave, Hagar most likely had no choice about participating in the scheme concocted by Sarah. Mr. and Mrs. Abraham were getting up there in years, and something had to be done in order to help God deliver the child promised to them. Hagar was pretty much an innocent victim in the matter. She was used by Sarah and Abraham and had little control in the matter.

Once Sarah turned on her, Hagar ran away. This time she had some degree of control and exercised it. For the moment, she was free from her mistress's abuse. What happened next, however, gives us some insight into Hagar's faith. When the Lord (via his angel) offered her the promise of many descendants and instructed her to return to Sarah, she obeyed. Even though it couldn't have been easy, Hagar believed in the Lord's promise of provision and returned to her mistress. Before she left, however, Hagar referred to the Lord by the Hebrew name of "*El-Roi*," the God who sees. Some Bible translations preserve this original title, gratefully spoken by a woman who was touched by the fact that God saw and cared about her suffering.

Once Ishmael was born, Hagar was of little use to Sarah. After her previous actions, it's not surprising that she eventually instructed Abraham to get rid of her. I find it interesting that God told Abraham to listen to his wife. Crazy? Maybe not. It could be another example of how God can work with an individual's free will. He doesn't have to change the way we act in order to bring good out of a situation. Whatever the reason may be, however, Hagar now found herself used and rejected. Once again, the circumstances were out of her control.

Alone in the wilderness with her son, Hagar was now in an even worse situation. In addition to everything else that had happened, she and Ishmael were now abandoned and helpless. When their water supply ran out, however, Hagar soon realized that someone didn't forget about them. Hearing their cries, the Lord intervened and provided them with life-saving water to drink. As we discussed in the previous section, that provision would continue into the future.

As he often does, God used a bad situation and the selfish actions of others to prove that he cares about the helpless. It may have appeared that Hagar was forgotten by everyone, but that was not the case. God was watching over her.

WHY IT MATTERS

The story of Hagar doesn't get a lot of attention, but its message is arguably one of the most important in all of scripture. Her life reminds us of the fact that nothing escapes the watchful eye of God. No matter how alone and abandoned we may feel, he is watching over us. There's no getting around the fact that people will use us and reject us at times. We may even get to the point where we are abandoned. Hagar's story assures us that God is never far from those who are helpless.

What happened to Hagar may seem a bit extreme, but I know a young woman who found herself in a very similar situation. Shortly after she gave birth, her husband left her and their son for another woman. While still dealing with the difficulties of delivering her first child, this young lady was suddenly thrown into the role of mother, single parent, and breadwinner. In addition to dealing with betrayal and rejection, she had to find an affordable place to live. Her story is still unfolding as I write this, but the Lord has made his presence known. Needs are being met and the family is being provided for. While there's no denying the evil and tragic events that took place, the Lord has gradually been bringing good out of a bad situation.

The world is filled with people who have been forgotten: abandoned spouses, refugees, prisoners, the homeless, shut-ins, and the mentally ill. The life of Hagar offers conclusive proof that God is aware of these individuals, even if nobody else is. Furthermore, the "God who sees" is willing and able to provide for their needs. His work in the life of a woman who was used, rejected, and abandoned illustrates just how caring "*El-Roi*" really is.

PRAYER

Dear *El-Roi*, you came to the assistance of Hagar after she was used, rejected, and abandoned. Seeing how you worked in her life helps me to understand that you truly are the "God who sees." Even though I sometimes feel that nobody cares about me, I now understand that this isn't the case. It's comforting to know that you're aware of my struggles and that you're always willing to help me. Thank you, *El-Roi*. Amen.

DISCUSSION QUESTIONS

1. What touched you the most about the story of Hagar?

2. Have you ever been used, rejected, or abandoned? How did it make you feel?

3. Identify someone who has been forgotten by others. How might God be able to work through you to help them? Try to develop a concrete plan to assist in some way. (Note: In addition to external actions, don't forget prayer. It's the most important thing you can do for someone in need.)

Chapter 8

WHEN YOU'RE NOT STRONG ENOUGH (PAUL)

2 Corinthians 12:1-10

Throughout my life, I have found myself in many uncomfortable situations. In most of the cases, I had no say in the matter. Things happened and I ended up somewhere I didn't want to be. While the particulars of each situation may have looked different, my prayers sounded remarkably similar. When turning to God after finding myself in the middle of an unwelcome challenge, my typical response is, "Lord, please make it go away."

If you think about it, it's a pretty reasonable approach. When something is causing me pain and I can't get rid of it, turning to the one who can do all things and asking him to fix it makes a lot of sense. It makes me feel better to know that Paul took the same approach. When dealing with his "thorn in the flesh," he asked the Lord to make it go away. Actually, he asked multiple times. God responded, but not by taking away the problem (2 Cor 12:7–10).

We have all been in Paul's position. We encounter a painful situation and ask God to make it better. He responds with a no and we feel defeated. Why wouldn't he grant our request? Mainly because he plans to bring a greater good out of it. Let's take a closer look at how this played out in the life of Paul.

THE FACTS

In this part of his Second Letter to the Corinthians, Paul speaks about visions and divine revelation. He writes about a man who had seen a very realistic and powerful vision of heaven "fourteen years ago" (2 Cor 12:2). In this vision, the individual heard things that "cannot be told" (2 Cor 12:4). Shifting gears, Paul goes on to state he will only boast of his weaknesses. Even though he wishes to boast, he will refrain from doing so.

As we read on, it becomes clear that the man who experienced these visions is most likely Paul himself. He writes that he was given a "thorn . . . in the flesh" in order to keep him from boasting about the "abundance of revelations" (2 Cor 12:7). We never learn whether this "thorn" was an illness, a physical disability (some have suggested failing eyesight), or a person, but we are told that it was given to him to keep him "from being too elated" (2 Cor 12:7).

Paul begged the Lord not once, not twice, but three times to take away this suffering. He received this response instead: "My grace is sufficient for you, for my power is made perfect in weakness" (2 Cor 12:9).

Something must have clicked when Paul heard these words, as he closes this discussion by returning to the previously mentioned topic of boasting. No longer referring to the supernatural visions, he proclaims his desire to boast of his weaknesses. Specifically, he makes the case that his weakness enables the power of Christ to come alive. Paul acknowledges that when he is weak, he becomes strong in Christ: "I will all the more gladly boast of my weaknesses, that the power of Christ may rest upon me. For the sake of Christ, then, I am content with weaknesses, insults, hardships, persecutions, and calamities; for when I am weak, then I am strong" (2 Cor 12:9–10).

Paul makes it clear that he is content to face whatever suffering comes his way. He understands that any situation that makes him feel weak is actually an opportunity for the strength of Christ to burst forth.

A CLOSER LOOK

When I look at the life of St. Paul, particularly his trials and accomplishments, the word "weak" doesn't immediately come to mind. In my opinion, he ranks up there as a superhero. Before I began to study his writings, I absolutely considered him to be totally out of my league. While he may still be light-years ahead of me in the strength department, the passage we're looking at in this chapter narrows the gap a little bit. Reading his words helps me to realize that Paul wasn't able to endure tremendous suffering and adversity because he was strong. He was able to do it because of the grace given to him by Jesus.

For the record, no matter what he wrote, Paul was not a weak person. Nobody would be able to endure the trials he suffered without toughness and resolve. Here's the takeaway from Paul's situation, however: no matter how strong any of us are, we are infinitely less powerful than Christ. According to worldly standards, Paul may have been considered strong—but not according to divine standards. Paul understood that concept well, which enabled him to boast of his weakness. It probably took time for him to arrive at this way of thinking, however, which leads me to the next part of our discussion.

Earlier in the chapter, I mentioned that my initial reaction to adversity is to pray that God will take it away. This is especially the case when my "thorn in the flesh" is getting in the way of my responsibilities. After all, it's a lot more difficult to write if I'm not feeling well. Giving a talk or leading a parish mission is so much easier when I've had a good night's sleep. With all that Paul had to get done, it's only logical for him to ask God to remove the "thorn in his flesh." And that's exactly what he did—three times. What may seem logical to us, however, isn't always logical to God.

One lesson we can learn from Paul is that God hears and answers our prayers. Furthermore, it's apparent that sometimes we need to pray more than once before we get a definitive answer. It's obvious that Paul didn't receive a concrete response the first two times, or he wouldn't have kept asking. Finally, Paul understood what the Lord was trying to tell him. Whether it came audibly or in the silence of his heart we don't know. What we do know, however, is that Paul finally understood that his painful "thorn in the flesh" was no match for the power of God's grace. That's a point that would have been very difficult, if not impossible, for Paul to understand if the thorn had been taken away.

WHY IT MATTERS

What I like most about this story, other than the reminder that God hears and answers our cries for help, is that it illustrates how we often put limits on the power of grace. While Paul provides justification for praying that the Lord will remove a problem, he also shows us how to respond when the answer is no.

As powerful as Paul's example may be, it's not entirely original. The Bible contains another illustration of an individual who, when faced with a serious problem, prayed in a similar way. On the night before he died, Jesus fell on his face and spoke these words to his Father: "My Father, if it be possible, let this chalice pass from me; nevertheless, not as I will, but as you will" (Mt 26:39).

I'm hesitant to read too much into this passionate plea from Jesus, but it's clear from his words that there's a difference between his human will and the will of his Father (*CCC*, 475). While his words can appear troubling at first, the sentiment he expressed gives us a model of how we should pray: Father, not my will, but your will be done.

After providing us with that example, Jesus took it to the next level when he repeated the prayer a second and a third time. As important as these examples of prayer are, however, Jesus teaches us an even more powerful lesson by his decision to do the will of his Father. This same pattern, from beginning to end, is evident in Paul's prayer: ask, ask again, accept the answer. Both Jesus and Paul acknowledged that the Father's answer is always best.

In order to have a healthy relationship with God and find peace in life, we need to adopt Paul's "when I am weak, I am strong" philosophy. Realistically speaking, that's easier said than done. As someone who likes to be in control, I tend to respond to a crisis by immediately jumping into action. If I truly believed in my weakness and God's power, however, shouldn't I always remember to pray first? Of course I should, but that's one of the problems we face. We forget how much we need God's help.

Fortunately, God recognizes this shortcoming and allows us to face situations that remind us of how weak we are. Paul's "thorn in the flesh" forced him to recognize his weakness and reminded him that he needed to rely on

God's help. Our own reminder might come in the form of cancer, poverty, a difficult coworker, limited mobility, or just about anything else. The thing to remember is, no matter how severely we are afflicted or how weak we may feel, God's power can come alive in us if we give up control and let him work.

PRAYER

Dear Jesus, I constantly find myself telling you how much I need you and then taking matters into my own hands as if you don't exist. Thank you for sending me various "thorns in the flesh" to help me remember how much I need your help. Please grant me the grace to deal with these difficulties by letting your power work in me. Help me to remember that whenever you deny my request to remove a problem, it's for my own good. Thank you for caring so much about me.
Amen.

DISCUSSION QUESTIONS

1. How do you typically react when experiencing a "thorn in the flesh"?

2. How does the prayer of Jesus on the night before he died express his love for the Father? Does the fact that Jesus appeared to desire a different outcome factor into this love in any way? (Hint: Focus on what Jesus *did*, not on how he *felt*.)

3. Why do you think God sometimes responds to our prayers by taking away the suffering, and other times he doesn't?

Chapter 9

WHEN YOU'RE PERSECUTED FOR YOUR FAITH (SHADRACH, MESHACH, AND ABEDNEGO)

Daniel 3:1-30

What comes to mind when you hear about religious persecution? While these words often conjure up images of armed government agents forcefully breaking up religious services and hauling worshippers off to prison, there are countless other ways that believers experience persecution on a daily basis. Make no mistake, violent and extreme religious persecution still exists in many locations around the world, but there are many subtle ways that we also experience it closer to home. Sadly, many of the most emotionally painful incidents occur inside our homes as spouses, children, or parents exert pressure on those who try to live as faithful followers of Jesus Christ.

I have spoken with many individuals who suffer persecution because of their religious beliefs. Whether this abuse comes in the form of sarcasm, angry comments, or threats of violence doesn't change the fact that it can be a painful and lonely experience. Even though it shouldn't come as a surprise, especially if we consider how Jesus was treated, continued persecution can drive us to avoid speaking out and instead go underground with our Christian beliefs.

Shadrach, Meshach, and Abednego were young Hebrew men who knew what it was like to experience religious persecution. Their situation was extreme, but it can serve as a valuable learning experience for anyone who encounters some form of persecution due to their religious beliefs. If God can bring good out of their situation, which he most definitely did, he can bring good out of whatever you're experiencing.

THE FACTS

King Nebuchadnezzar, who reigned over Babylon, created a golden image and commanded all people to bow down and worship it. It was soon brought to his attention, however, that three young men refused to obey his instructions. Initially brought to Babylon after Nebuchadnezzar's defeat of Jerusalem, Shadrach, Meshach, and Abednego now found themselves in big trouble with the king. Nebuchadnezzar was enraged and summoned the men to appear before him.

He asked them if it was true that they refused to bow before the golden image and worship his gods, but didn't wait for them to answer. Instead, the king gave them another chance to put aside their religious beliefs and bow before his golden image. He also provided some incentive by threatening to cast them into a fiery furnace if they didn't comply. Nebuchadnezzar concluded his diatribe by demanding the name of the god who would be able to deliver them out of his hands. Their reply made clear exactly how they felt and what they planned to do:

> O Nebuchadnez'zar, we have no need to answer you in this matter. If it be so, our God whom we serve is able to deliver us from the burning fiery furnace; and he will deliver us out of your hand, O king. But if not, be it known to you, O king, that we will not serve your gods or worship the golden image which you have set up. (Dn 3:16–18)

Their response infuriated the king, and he ordered that the furnace be heated seven times hotter than normal. Then Nebuchadnezzar had the three men bound and thrown into the furnace. After carrying out the king's order, the servants who tossed Shadrach, Meshach, and Abednego into the fire were themselves killed by the extra-hot flames.

Instead of being incinerated, however, the three men in the furnace were protected by God. As they walked about unharmed in the flames, they sang hymns and blessed the Lord. King Nebuchadnezzar was astonished by what he saw as he peered into the furnace. He saw not three but four men walking around in the fire, all of whom were unharmed. He noted that the fourth man was like "a son of the gods" (Dn 3:25).

The king called Shadrach, Meshach, and Abednego out of the fire, whereupon all present could see no evidence of them being burned. The astonished King Nebuchadnezzar responded by saying: "Blessed be the God of Shadrach, Meshach, and Abednego, who has sent his angel and delivered his servants, who trusted in him, and set at nothing the king's command, and yielded up their bodies rather than serve and worship any god except their own God" (Dn 3:28). The king then decreed that anyone speaking badly about the God of Shadrach, Meshach, and Abednego would be cut into pieces and have their house destroyed. The three men were then promoted to higher positions in the province of Babylon.

A CLOSER LOOK

It's hard to comprehend how God could use religious persecution to his advantage, but that's exactly what happened in this story from the book of Daniel. Even though the actions of Nebuchadnezzar are undeniably evil, the Lord permitted him to carry them out. Why? You guessed it! Once again, God will use them to bring about a greater good.

When You're Persecuted for Your Faith (Shadrach, Meshach, and Abednego)

Let's begin by looking at why Shadrach, Meshach, and Abednego were in Babylon in the first place. They were there because the power-hungry Nebuchadnezzar chose to conquer Jerusalem and deport many of its inhabitants to his country. We don't know why God allowed this to happen, but we can see an important subplot taking place. God would use King Nebuchadnezzar's actions to bring about his conversion.

After they were exiled from their homes, the three Hebrew men's faith was put to the test in Babylon. When the king ordered all of his subjects to do something that violated their religious beliefs, Shadrach, Meshach, and Abednego were forced to make a choice. Even though they undoubtedly knew there would be repercussions, the three men chose to disobey the king and remain faithful to God. As could be anticipated, Nebuchadnezzar didn't take well to their disobedience.

In an action that would be expected from a power-hungry and controlling ruler, the king tried to force them into obedience by threatening them with a gruesome punishment. The devout young men were not deterred by this act of religious persecution, and they refused to compromise their beliefs. At this point, Nebuchadnezzar was far from any kind of conversion and was filled with fury.

After ordering that the men be thrown into the furnace, the king watched as Shadrach, Meshach, and Abednego praised God and walked unharmed in the flames. (As an aside, the song of praise sung by the three men in the fire is interspersed in this story and only appears in Catholic translations of the Bible. It is a great example of divine praise, and I highly recommend that you take the time to read and pray it.) Rising up in astonishment, Nebuchadnezzar claimed that he saw a fourth man in the fire. Although it's not explicitly stated in the narrative, this figure indicates God's protection of the three men.

King Nebuchadnezzar commanded the men to get out of the fire; he could no longer deny the undeniable. Recognizing the God of Shadrach, Meshach, and Abednego, he decreed that anyone who speaks against their God would have their house destroyed and be subject to dismemberment. In the end, aside from any deepening of faith experienced by the men in the fire, this blatant act of religious persecution resulted in the conversion of a power-hungry, idol-worshipping ruler. It may sound like a convoluted plan to us, but God's ways are not our ways. Even if we don't understand his methods, it's pretty hard to argue with that kind of success.

WHY IT MATTERS

I may never have the experience of being physically tortured or imprisoned because of my religious beliefs, but I definitely know what it feels like to be belittled, misunderstood, and ignored because I have chosen to follow Jesus. The odds are good that you know what it's like too. While I would never freely choose to experience this type of treatment, I have to admit that it has its benefits.

When You're Persecuted for Your Faith (Shadrach, Meshach, and Abednego)

Every instance of religious persecution can be viewed as an opportunity. When faced with opposition or potential opposition to our beliefs, we can choose to exercise our trust in God and his faithfulness. Just like the three Hebrew men who didn't know for certain that they would survive the deadly flames, we can decide to place our trust in God even if the outcome isn't guaranteed. Making this decision, even if we're afraid, almost always impacts our faith in a positive way. There have been many times when I chose to take the path of least resistance and remained silent in the face of potential opposition, but I have never regretted those occasions when I made the decision to stand firm.

In addition to the benefits we experience personally, how we react to religious persecution can have a positive impact on those around us. Over the course of my life, I have been greatly inspired by many individuals who boldly proclaimed their faith in Jesus Christ and his Church, sometimes at great cost. Watching them in action often made me question my own cowardly behavior. And this is not just something that happened in the distant past. I still experience it from time to time, and I'm grateful that I do. Those incidents challenge me and inspire me to become a better witness for the Lord in a world that is very much in need of witnesses.

Finally, as was clearly seen in the case of King Nebuchadnezzar, religious persecution can even bring about a conversion in the individual doing the persecuting. It's difficult to accept this when you're the one being persecuted, but God cares just as much about the one dishing it out as he does about you. He wants that individual to be converted, and you may be the instrument he uses to make it happen. Standing firm in the face of religious persecution has a way of inspiring others, but be patient. It took a lot for King Nebuchadnezzar to see the light, but it did happen. Your spouse, child, coworker, boss, or neighbor may seem to be a lost cause, but that is never the case. Pray for the grace to do the right thing, and leave the rest up to God. As evidenced by the case of Shadrach, Meshach, and Abednego, God can always bring good out of religious persecution.

PRAYER

Dear Holy Spirit, sometimes I can be cowardly when it comes to standing up for my faith. With your help, however, I can overcome my spirit of cowardice and act in a powerful way that pleases you and inspires others. Grant me the grace to make the best of this opportunity, letting your power flow through me. Help me always to remember that I am never alone, even if it feels that way at times. I ask this of you in the mighty name of Jesus Christ, who lives and reigns with

you and the Father—God, forever and ever.
Amen.

DISCUSSION QUESTIONS

1. Have you ever backed down when faced with the threat of religious persecution? Did anything positive come from your behavior in those situations?

2. What enabled Shadrach, Meshach, and Abednego to act in the way they acted? How does their behavior make you feel?

3. In what ways can you identify with King Nebuchadnezzar and his behavior? (Note: This is a very tough question. Give it plenty of thought!)

Chapter 10

WHEN YOU'RE HIDING IN FEAR (APOSTLES IN UPPER ROOM)

John 20:19-29

Even with my long history of worrying and catastrophizing, I was unable to imagine how the COVID-19 pandemic would turn our world upside down. March of 2020 started normally enough—I had a full Lenten speaking schedule ahead of me. That schedule and my life began to derail on March 12 when the previously unheard of COVID-19 virus began to rear its ugly head. One by one, events began to be canceled. When I heard the news that the NBA and Broadway were shutting down, I knew that this was serious. Sure enough, all of my remaining speaking engagements were canceled, one by one. For a full-time speaker and author like me, that was a very big problem. What I didn't know at the time, however, was that it was about to get worse.

Never before in my life had I faced a situation where I found myself literally hiding in fear. I had plenty of experience dealing with threatening situations, real and imaginary, but never anything like this. My family and I were literally hiding in the house, trying to protect ourselves from an unknown and rapidly intensifying threat that appeared to be all around us. Cut off from the world, we desperately tried to find hope in the midst of what increasingly appeared to be a hopeless situation.

After the death of Jesus, the apostles knew that they were "marked men." Seeing what had happened to their master, they had every reason to believe they were next in line. As a result, they did what seemed logical to them—they locked the door and hid from those who put Jesus to death. As we'll soon discover, though, what appeared to be a hopeless situation turned around in an instant. It all happened when a very special person came to visit, bringing with him a priceless gift: peace.

THE FACTS

On the evening of the day when Jesus rose from the dead, the apostles were hiding with the doors shut "for fear of the Jews," when Jesus came and stood among them. Speaking the words "Peace be with you," he showed them his hands and his side (Jn 20:19). They had not seen him since he was crucified and, as you could imagine, they were filled with joy.

Repeating the words "Peace be with you," Jesus gave his followers an important mission. He informed them that they would be the ones continuing his work in the world. Jesus was sending them to spread God's kingdom, just as the Father sent him. He then breathed on them and said, "Receive the Holy Spirit. If you forgive the sins of any, they are forgiven; if you retain the sins of any, they are retained" (Jn 20:21–23).

Thomas, one of the Twelve, was not with them on that day. When the others told him that they had seen the Lord, he refused to believe. Thomas insisted that he would only believe if he could see the Lord's nail prints and touch his wounds.

Eight days later, the apostles were gathered in the same room, and this time Thomas was with them. Once again the doors were shut, and once again Jesus appeared, delivering a familiar message: "Peace be with you" (Jn 20:26). Speaking directly to Thomas, the Lord invited the skeptical apostle to touch his hands and side. Thomas answered with the familiar words that have been repeated so many times through the ages: "My Lord and my God!" (Jn 20:28).

A CLOSER LOOK

There's no denying the fact that the apostles were not in a good place after the death of Jesus. When this narrative begins, we find them hiding behind locked doors "for fear of the Jews" (Jn 20:19). Even though Jesus had risen from the dead, his disciples were living as if he was still in the tomb. By locking the doors and hiding from what frightened them, the eleven remaining apostles (minus Thomas) attempted to carve out a safe place and find some degree of peace.

Knowing that his followers needed peace, Jesus sought them out. While the Bible doesn't specifically state that Jesus passed through a locked door (John simply writes that the doors were shut), Luke's account states that the disciples were "startled and frightened" (Lk 24:37) when Jesus appeared and thought they were seeing a spirit. Whatever the case may have been, the Lord's first words to them were, "Peace be with you" (Jn 20:19). After showing them his hands and side, something clicked and they "were glad when they saw the Lord" (Jn 20:20). Once again, he repeated the message of peace.

After delivering his message and letting his followers examine his wounds, Jesus breathed on them and gave them the authority to forgive sins in his name. The Church has typically viewed this as the institution of the Sacrament of Confession, which often brings the same peace that the apostles received in that locked room.

Thomas was not with the others when the Lord appeared and refused to believe their account of what took place. It has often been speculated that Thomas's absence was due to a crisis of faith, but that may or may not be the case. What is important is that Jesus made a point to return to the same house eight days later when Thomas was present. Addressing the skeptical apostle directly, Jesus gave him a chance to touch his hands and side. Even though it's commonly assumed that Thomas took Jesus up on his offer and touched his wounds, the Bible is actually silent on the matter. What we do know conclusively, however, is that something about the Lord's appearance to Thomas caused his faith to solidify as he proclaimed Jesus as his Lord and his God.

Before we move on and discuss why all of this matters, I want to sum up what I consider to be the main takeaway from this story. Between Thomas's skepticism and Jesus giving his apostles the authority to forgive sins, it's easy to lose sight of the big picture. The apostles were hiding out because they were afraid, and Jesus appeared to them and brought them peace. He found a way to break through their fear and give them hope. Even when Thomas resisted, Jesus didn't give up on him. He made a return visit, specifically targeting the one who doubted. His actions call to mind the parable of the lost sheep (Mt 18:10–14), when the shepherd leaves the ninety-nine to find the one who was lost. Jesus didn't stop until all the apostles understood that he rose from the dead and is alive. It was a concept they needed to understand in order to move forward.

WHY IT MATTERS

Because of my personal experience in the early days of the pandemic, I can definitely relate to the story of the frightened apostles hiding behind closed doors. I'm happy to report, however, that the similarity doesn't end there. Like the apostles, my family and I knew what it was like to have Jesus visit us as we were locked down at home. Through the online Mass, Bible reading, and coming together in prayer, the Lord found a way to comfort us and decrease our fear. Eventually, this enabled us to venture out into the world and gradually resume our pre-COVID lives.

Given the fact that we experienced a global pandemic in our lifetime, the idea of hiding in fear behind locked doors is very relatable. But it's important to note that this kind of fear doesn't always lead to that actual experience—it is entirely possible to be out in the world, figuratively hiding in fear at the same time. Every day we are bombarded with an endless stream of messages telling us why we should be afraid: an approaching storm, a new illness, increased violence, higher cost of living, product shortages, and so on. Not a day goes by without someone reminding us that we should be afraid. It's not surprising that we sometimes give in and become overwhelmed with fear.

The story of the apostles hiding behind locked doors provides conclusive evidence that Jesus will seek us out and offer peace when we are consumed by fear. And, as illustrated by the story of Thomas, he'll keep trying. Ultimately, however, it's up to us to make a choice. We can either listen to the world or we can listen to Jesus. When he appeared to the terrified apostles, the Lord didn't remove the external threat. There were still plenty of people who wanted to kill these men. Rather, he gave them peace in the middle of the storm and provided them with the confidence they needed to unlock the doors and venture out into the world.

PRAYER

Dear Jesus, there are so many reasons to be afraid right now, but I choose to focus on the fact that you are with me. Even though I know that you are bigger than any problem I could ever face, I don't always feel it in my heart. Sometimes I feel like Thomas, Lord. I want to believe in you, but I have so many doubts, and my problems seem so large. Please come to me and make your presence known in some way. In the meantime, I'll choose to trust in you no matter how I feel. Amen.

DISCUSSION QUESTIONS

1. Did the apostles have a valid reason to be afraid? How about after Jesus appeared to them?

2. Do you think it coincidental that Jesus showed up when Thomas was absent? Why or why not? Why does it matter to you?

3. How do you feel about the "doubting Thomas" nickname? Is it fair, or does it overlook some of the positive aspects of Thomas's faith?

Chapter 11

WHEN YOU'VE MADE A BAD DECISION (JONAH)

Jonah 1-4

I'm not especially fond of making decisions. Sadly, I'm not just talking about major decisions, but the minor ones as well. It's not out of the question for me to stare at a restaurant menu, going back and forth as to what I should choose. Much of my indecisiveness comes from my tendency to overthink everything and go to extreme measures to avoid negative consequences. If I'm struggling to choose between the roast beef sandwich ("It could be too chewy") and the cheeseburger ("What if it's too well done?"), try to imagine how difficult it is for me to buy a car, change jobs, or try to discern God's will.

For me, it all comes down to a fear of making a bad decision. What will happen if I make the wrong choice? With my well-documented history as a worst-case thinker, there never seems to be a shortage of "wrong choices" running around in my head. As a result, I have often avoided making major decisions. More often than not, I have chosen to play it safe so that nothing can go wrong. Even if that were true (which it isn't), I have come to understand that this way of thinking completely denies the fact that God can bring good out of even the worst decision.

Jonah was handpicked by the Lord for an important mission, but he refused and tried to run away instead. In a very dramatic and memorable way, God gave him a chance to reconsider. The story is so familiar and the details are so extraordinary, however, that the overall message is often unnoticed. Let's take a closer look at how God's will can still move forward, even when the person he's counting on makes a really bad decision.

THE FACTS

The book of Jonah opens with the Lord instructing Jonah to travel to the Assyrian city of Nineveh and call for the people to repent from their wickedness. Jonah responded by running away from God and boarding a boat for Tarshish, which was in the opposite direction. After the boat set sail, God sent a storm that created a dangerous situation for those on board. The members of the crew were afraid and cast lots to find out who was responsible for the calamity. They were led to Jonah.

After admitting to the crew that he was running from the Lord, Jonah asked to be thrown overboard. By doing so, he believed that the storm would cease. Jonah was cast into the sea and the storm subsided, as expected. The Lord sent a "great fish" (Jon 1:17) to swallow Jonah, who remained in its belly for three days and three nights. After thanking God for sparing his life, Jonah was vomited out by the fish onto dry land. Then God commanded Jonah for the second time to travel to Nineveh, and this time he obeyed. Arriving in the city, Jonah proclaimed the message that the Lord gave him: "Yet forty days, and Nineveh shall be overthrown!" (Jon 3:4).

The people heeded the prophet's warning and repented, proclaiming a fast and putting on sackcloth. When word reached the king of Nineveh, he decreed that all should fast and cry out to God. It was his belief that the people's repentance might cause the Lord to have mercy on them. That is exactly what happened.

Even though he was the one who delivered God's message, Jonah was not happy that the Ninevites were spared. He was so upset that he begged God to take his life. The story ends with the Lord lecturing Jonah about his lack of mercy. We don't know what happened to him, but we do know that God's will prevailed. The people of Nineveh repented of their wickedness, and it happened because of the message delivered, albeit reluctantly, by Jonah.

A CLOSER LOOK

In the second verse of the book of Jonah, we read about the prophet being given an important mission from the Lord. The people of Nineveh were engaging in some sort of unspecified wickedness, and God wanted to give them a chance to repent. It soon became clear that Jonah had no intention of obeying the Lord's instructions. He boarded a ship headed to Tarshish in the opposite direction. Jonah had decided to disobey God.

Because he didn't want to give up on the Ninevites, however, God sent a storm to thwart Jonah's planned escape. It's also interesting to note that the Lord was able to use the crew's superstitious practice of casting lots to lead them to Jonah as the cause of the storm. Once confronted, Jonah owned up and asked to be thrown into the sea. Before doing so, however, the pagan crew experienced a conversion (a foreshadowing of what we'll see with the Ninevites) and begged God to forgive them for what they were about to do.

The Lord sent a great fish to swallow Jonah. He remained inside the fish for three days and three nights, which gave him plenty of time to reflect on his decision to disobey God. Realizing that the Lord was responsible for saving his life, Jonah offered a prayer of thanksgiving. Once the whale (although it's never clearly specified in the Bible, it's likely what is meant by "great fish"!) spit out Jonah on dry land, he decided to head to Nineveh after all. Just as is often the case with us, Jonah needed a little extra convincing before choosing to listen to God.

Once in Nineveh, Jonah carried out his mission—no more, no less. It's obvious that his heart wasn't in it, because his message was totally devoid of hope or compassion. He simply told the people that they would be destroyed in forty days. Despite Jonah's lack of sincerity, however, the Ninevites took the words to heart and repented of their sinfulness. Mission accomplished. Despite Jonah's initial bad decision and his continued bad attitude, God accomplished what he set out to do.

There are bad decisions and there are *bad* decisions. Choosing to deliberately disobey God, as Jonah did, definitely falls into the latter category. Even so, however, he was given another chance to obey the Lord and carry out an important mission. He did so reluctantly, but God was still able to use his effort to bring about the repentance of the Ninevites. Ultimately, bad decisions and even bad attitudes aren't enough to stop God from accomplishing his will. That is really excellent news.

WHY IT MATTERS

In order to truly appreciate the message contained in the story of Jonah, it's important to put aside the whole "swallowed by a whale" narrative and focus on the big picture. This is a story of God's message being delivered and responded to, even though he used a messenger who made a really bad decision and had a really bad attitude.

In the end, the story of Jonah offers proof that the Lord can bring good out of any bad decision we ever make. It is a story of hope.

Just like Jonah, I have said no to God many times. Sometimes it was because of sin, and other times I was afraid or unwilling to do what he was calling me to do. Whatever the case, Jonah's story reminds me that my imperfections aren't enough to thwart God's plans. Not only does it take away some of the pressure ("What if I do the wrong thing?") in the present, but it takes away the guilt ("I messed everything up!") caused by my past mistakes. If the Lord can bring good out of Jonah's situation, he can do the same with mine.

It's been said that God writes straight with crooked lines. He certainly did so with Jonah. Every one of us has made at least one bad decision in the past. Don't give yourself too much credit. No matter how badly you messed up, you're not powerful enough to foil God's plans. Just ask Jonah.

PRAYER

Dear God, thank you for giving me the story of Jonah. Even though I have said no to you and made some bad decisions in the past, his story reminds me that you can still use me for good. My attitude hasn't been the greatest at times, but you already know that. I want to turn things around. As you proved with Jonah, you can work with all of my imperfections and attitude issues as long as I say yes. I can't change what I did in the past, but I can try to do the right thing now. I'm grateful to have another chance. I'll do whatever you ask of me. Amen.

DISCUSSION QUESTIONS

1. Are you afraid of making a bad decision? Why or why not?

2. What did you learn from the story of Jonah? How will it affect the way you approach making decisions in the future?

3. Discuss what Jonah did right and what he did wrong. How did his actions affect the lives of others?

Chapter 12

WHEN THERE'S NO END TO YOUR SUFFERING (WOMAN WITH A HEMORRHAGE)

Mark 5:25-34

How's your confidence level when you pray? It's been my experience that I feel most confident when I initially present my intentions to the Lord. As time goes on and I don't get what I want, however, my confidence level begins to decrease. This is a very common occurrence—the longer we pray for something, the harder it is to believe that God will grant our request.

In his gospel, Mark records the story of a woman who had every reason to believe that she wouldn't be healed. Not only had she been sick for twelve years, but she had some other very big problems as well. When faced with what appeared to be a hopeless future, however, she managed to cling to the belief that things could turn around for her. There may have been no end in sight, but sometimes it's not about seeing. In her case, it was all about faith. She had it, she used it, and she was healed. Her story warrants a closer look.

THE FACTS

When Jesus landed on the other side of the Sea of Galilee, he was met by a great crowd of people. One of the rulers of the synagogue, Jairus, fell at his feet and begged Jesus to heal his daughter. Accompanied by the crowd, Jesus went with the synagogue official. While on the way, however, they encountered a woman who had been suffering from a flow of blood for twelve years. According to Mark's account, she had "suffered much under many physicians, and had spent all that she had, and was no better but rather grew worse" (Mk 5:26).

Undaunted by her situation, this unnamed woman heard about Jesus, sought him out, came up behind him, and touched his garment. She believed that if she only touched his clothes, she would be healed of her disease. As she anticipated, that's exactly what happened. She was cured immediately. Feeling that power had left his body, Jesus asked who it was that touched him. The disciples tried to downplay the comment because of the large crowd, but Jesus was determined to find out who had touched his garments. As he turned, Jesus saw the woman falling down before him. In fear and trembling, she told him that she was the one who had touched him.

Jesus closed out this encounter by saying, "Daughter, your faith has made you well; go in peace, and be healed of your disease" (Mk 5:34).

After this, Jesus went back to the business of healing Jairus's daughter. The woman who was healed after twelve years is never mentioned again.

A CLOSER LOOK

Embedded within the story of Jesus healing the daughter of Jairus is the tale of a woman who appeared to be in a hopeless situation. Even though her story is recorded in three of the gospels (Matthew, Mark, and Luke), we never learn her name or any other biographical details about her. What we do learn, however, is what the Holy Spirit considers to be the important details. We know that she had suffered from a flow of blood (a hemorrhage) for twelve years and that she had spent all that she had on multiple physicians. Not only did she not get better, but her condition deteriorated. Things couldn't get much worse, right? Wrong!

As documented in Leviticus 15:25, this medical condition rendered her unclean. In addition to her physical suffering and poverty, that meant she could have no contact with others. For twelve years, she was an outcast, and there was no end in sight. Even if she could find another physician, the woman had no money. Her future looked bleak, but she somehow found enough hope to consider another option. It was one that even she could afford, as it didn't cost anything.

At some point during this time, she came to believe that Jesus could heal her. For all we know, she could have come to this conclusion the day before she met him. We simply don't know when it occurred. One thing is clear, however: she never totally gave up hope. Other people may have thrown in the towel if they were in her situation, but she did not. That proved to be a very wise decision.

Taking a break from the hemorrhaging woman, let's focus on Jesus for a minute. We can learn something about him by looking at how he acted in this situation. Even though he was responding to an urgent problem and surrounded by people, he felt the touch of this desperate woman and stopped to acknowledge her. This serves as proof that he's never too busy to respond to someone who reaches out to him—even if that someone is rejected by everyone else.

Take note of the fact that the woman didn't even have to say anything to Jesus in order to be healed. All that was required was the desire to touch him and the belief that he could heal her. When she approached him with humility from behind (remember, she was forbidden to have contact with others), she was healed immediately. According to Jesus, she was healed because of her faith. What would have happened if she gave up and stopped believing that her hopeless situation could turn around? We don't know. But no matter how bleak things may have looked, her faith in Jesus was rewarded and she was healed.

WHY IT MATTERS

Unless we exercise some caution, we can get so distracted by the details of this story that we lose sight of the practical application. Your hopeless situation may have nothing to do with a twelve-year flow of blood, and it may not involve spending all of your money on doctors, but what happened here is relevant for anyone who is suffering with no end in sight.

The story reminds us of the importance of never giving up hope, no matter how hopeless things look. As was made evident in the story of the hemorrhaging woman, Jesus can instantly transform your situation. While it's impossible to predict exactly how he will intervene, turning to him will always make things better. That "better" may happen externally (as in the case of the bleeding woman), or it may happen internally. Whether he eliminates the problem or changes you internally, things always get better once he is involved.

As I noted earlier in the chapter, the longer you pray and fail to see the results you want, the greater the temptation is to give up. Satan is well aware of this and will try to exploit the situation to his advantage. Don't be surprised when discouraging thoughts fill your mind and your situation feels hopeless. Fortunately, feelings aren't facts. You may not see an end to your suffering, but that doesn't mean that there isn't one. The story of the hemorrhaging woman reminds us of why we should never lose hope. Even if the world can't provide a solution to your problem, Jesus can. Sometimes, as in this case, it takes time. By all means, keep trying the conventional solutions to your problem, but don't forget about Jesus. As this desperate woman learned, sometimes all it takes is to touch the hem of his garment.

PRAYER

Dear Jesus, I'm suffering, and there doesn't seem to be an end in sight. Even though I know you can do all things, I'm having a hard time believing it. It's been a long time, and nothing seems to be changing. As the story of the woman with the hemorrhage reminds me, however, you can turn things around in an instant. Please grant me the grace to imitate this woman and keep hoping that things can turn around. Even if I don't feel it, I know that there is hope. Amen.

DISCUSSION QUESTIONS

1. Have you ever felt that something was hopeless, but then it somehow worked out? What can you learn from that experience?

2. Why do you think our prayers aren't always answered quickly?

3. What does this story teach you about Jesus? (Try to think of something in addition to his ability to heal.)

Chapter 13

WHEN YOU'RE STRUGGLING FINANCIALLY (ELIJAH AND THE WIDOW)

1 Kings 17:1-16

For the first several decades of my life, I gave very little thought to financial matters. I worried about many other things but had the privilege of having a place to live and food to eat. My parents were not wealthy by any means, but we lived in a single home in the suburbs and always had plenty of food and lived comfortably. We took vacations, went out to eat, and didn't want for much. That trend continued when I graduated from college and began a thirty-year career in the software industry. I wouldn't say I lived a life of luxury, but for the most part I was able to buy whatever I wanted.

Things began to change somewhat after Eileen and I got married and had children. I became more conscious of our limited resources and began to worry about what happened if I lost my job. Unlike before, when I depended on my parents or substantial savings, I was now the sole provider for my family, and we were living paycheck to paycheck. Even though I was concerned about finances, however, it still wasn't a huge issue for me.

That changed in a big way when I got laid off in 2012 and entered into full-time ministry. Suddenly, the words "give us this day our daily bread" took on a whole new meaning as we struggled to pay our bills. For the first time in my life, I realized that I was totally dependent on God's provision. It was a frightening realization.

In chapter 17 of 1 Kings, we are introduced to a prophet named Elijah. He appears on the scene abruptly and, after delivering a difficult message to the reigning king, is sent by God to a remote location. While there, Elijah is forced to depend totally on God's providence until he is sent to another location where he would be asked to depend on the Lord to an even greater extent. It's a story of how the Father provides for his children—not only spiritually, but materially as well.

THE FACTS

Elijah was a prophet who seemingly appeared out of nowhere to deliver an ominous message from God to King Saul. He informed the king that there would be no rain in the land until further notice. Specifically, Elijah proclaimed that the drought would last until he himself gave the word to end it. It was a bold proclamation and one that would surely anger the king, but we aren't given a chance to hear the king's response. Immediately after we read Elijah's words, the Bible tells us that God sent him eastward to hide by a stream, where he would find drinking water and be fed by ravens. Elijah obeyed.

As promised, the prophet was provided with drinking water and food. The water came from the stream, and his food (bread and meat) was delivered by ravens in the morning and evening. One day, however, the stream dried up, and God once more spoke to Elijah. He ordered him to travel to Zarephath, in Sidon, where the Lord had instructed a widow to provide for his needs. Elijah once again obeyed and traveled to Zarephath, where he encountered a widow at the gate of the city.

Acting on God's promise, Elijah called out to her and asked for water. As she was going inside to get it, he also asked for some bread. The woman told him that she had nothing baked, only a handful of meal and some oil. She went on to inform Elijah that she was on her way to gather some sticks to prepare a final meal for herself and her son. Despite hearing the shocking news, he persisted and asked that she take care of his needs first. He also added this important piece of information: "For thus says the Lord the God of Israel, 'The jar of meal shall not be spent, and the pitcher of oil shall not fail, until the day that the Lord sends rain upon the earth'" (1 Kgs 17:14).

The widow obeyed and did as Elijah said. As promised by the Lord, the jar of meal and the pitcher of oil did not run out. According to the Bible, she, Elijah, and her son went on to eat for "many days" (1 Kgs 17:15).

A CLOSER LOOK

This story, which took place at the beginning of Elijah's prophetic ministry, is not just an example of God's care for us, but a *radical* example of divine providence. Not only did God meet the needs of Elijah and the widow, but he filled them in an incredible way. At the heart of this story is a complete and total trust in the faithfulness of God. Both of the individuals who were involved were called to trust when conventional wisdom would tell them just the opposite. Because they trusted, however, they got to experience firsthand the provision of God. Let's examine exactly how God took care of them.

The minute that Elijah appeared before King Saul, announced a drought, and proclaimed that God put him in charge of future rainfall, he made himself a marked man. As a faithful worshipper of the idol Baal, Saul believed that the weather was controlled by his false god, and he wouldn't have taken kindly to the thought of someone else claiming that power. Before the king could react, however, Elijah was sent by God to a stream located east of the Jordan River.

The prophet was definitely in a precarious position but, as promised by God, his needs were being met. He was getting his drinking water from the stream and his food was being delivered to him morning and night by ravens. What is especially noteworthy about this is that ravens are birds of prey who do not voluntarily give up their food. The fact that God chose them to deliver food to Elijah is unusual, to say the least. It would take a great deal of trust for someone to believe that it could happen. Elijah believed, and God provided.

When the stream dried up because of the lack of rain (remember that there's still a drought going on), Elijah had no source of drinking water. Once more, God came to the rescue. He sent the prophet to Zarephath, a village located in Sidon. He was to look for a widow who would provide for his needs. The fact that God chose someone who had nothing to provide for someone else who also had nothing is yet another example of how he operates. He can provide for our needs in ways we can't comprehend. Once again, Elijah didn't overanalyze the Lord's plan. He obeyed, and God provided.

Taking God at his word, Elijah found the widow and boldly asked for something to drink and eat. She hesitated, informing him that she and her son were about to consume their last bit of food before they would die. Now, here's where things get really crazy. Elijah repeated his request, adding that their measly food supply would not run out. Amazingly, she believed him and did as he said. And guess what happened? They all continued to eat for "many days" (1 Kgs 17:15). Thus, we see yet another example of God providing for the needs of his creatures in a radical way.

What inspires me about this story is the fact that Elijah and the widow were completely incapable of providing for their own needs. Yet the Lord intervened and offered to help, in a way that seemed downright crazy. Both Elijah and the widow chose to trust, however, and God did just as he said. Everything about this story is extreme, but that's what makes it so inspiring. The Lord provided for two helpless people (three, if you include the widow's son) in a way that could only be pulled off by someone who could do the impossible. That's God for you!

WHY IT MATTERS

While most of us know (or will know) what it's like to struggle financially, very few of us will be able to comprehend the extent of trust required by Elijah and the widow. But that's exactly what makes their story so relevant. If God came through for them, we can trust that he'll come through for us as well.

I'm not about to try to make myself look good at the expense of the truth—I like being comfortable. I don't exactly look back fondly on my early days in ministry when I often had no idea how I'd be able to pay my monthly bills. It wasn't easy for me to depend on the Lord for my material needs. I never had a problem leaning on him for spiritual matters, but financial dependence was another story entirely. I may not have liked relying on God in this way, but I needed it. Furthermore, I'm grateful that it happened.

Having to count on the Lord to provide for the material needs of my family taught me a valuable lesson that would otherwise be extremely difficult to learn. God is faithful, and he will provide for the needs of his children. There is a catch, however, and it's an important one. The Lord will provide for our needs, but not necessarily for our wants. And sometimes it's very difficult to tell the difference. Over the course of the past decade, my family and I have found it necessary to cut back. In addition to the minor cutbacks (eating out, entertainment, and vacations), we made the decision to sell our single home and move into a mobile home. It was difficult at first, but it got easier. Not only did it enable me to continue in full-time ministry, but it helped my entire family appreciate the value of simple living. We are all grateful that we made the move.

If you're struggling to make ends meet, let the story of Elijah and the widow speak to you. God may not send wildlife to deliver food to you, but he is asking you to trust him as Elijah did. Elijah didn't quit the work he was given to do, but he did put God first. God took care of the rest.

The story we looked at in this chapter took place in the beginning of Elijah's ministry. Learning to depend on the Lord for his basic needs prepared him for what lay ahead. In order to do great things as a prophet, he first needed to have confidence in God's provision. That training took place beside a stream while being fed by ravens and with a helpless widow in Zarephath.

It's very uncomfortable to recognize that you can't provide for your own basic needs. Sometimes God is speaking to us in the circumstances of our lives. If we can't make ends meet, we shouldn't wait for God to miraculously send us money. We might have to make some hard choices. But if we put God first—even above our own material comfort—then we won't be in it alone. That process of surrender helps us understand just how much we need God.

If you're reading this right now, the Lord has provided for all of your needs from the time you were first conceived. Otherwise, you wouldn't be alive. One of the attributes of God is that he is immutable, which means that he doesn't change. If he provided for your needs in the past, you can be confident that he will do so in the future.

PRAYER

Dear Holy Spirit, I need your help right now. Please help me to believe that my heavenly Father will help me provide for my material needs. I want to have the faith of Elijah and the widow, but it's not easy for me. I'm so used to being self-sufficient that I feel powerless. When I pray, "Give us this day our daily bread," it feels as if I'm just going through the motions. I know that God provided for Elijah and the widow, but will he really do the same for me? Help me to believe it in my head and feel it in my heart. Finally, please let me know if I'm supposed to make lifestyle changes or seek additional sources of income. Amen.

DISCUSSION QUESTIONS

1. Why do you think Elijah and the widow were able to trust that God would provide for their needs?

2. What are some obstacles to recognizing your need for the Lord's provision in your life?

3. How might God be inviting you to participate in his providence by being a source of support for someone in need?

Chapter 14

WHEN YOU'RE GRIEVING THE DEATH OF A LOVED ONE (WIDOW OF NAIN)

Luke 7:11-17; John 16:16-24

One of the most difficult tasks we ever face is trying to find the right words to say to someone who is grieving the death of a loved one. Undoubtedly, many people arrive at the conclusion that there are no right words, and they simply choose to silently accompany those who are grieving. While I definitely see the value in this approach, I also believe that there are words that can ease the suffering of those who have experienced a loss.

In this chapter, I'll take a slightly different approach than what you've seen thus far. We'll begin by looking at an encounter between Jesus and a widow who was grieving the loss of her son. After examining Luke's account of how Jesus handled this particular situation, we'll jump over to John's gospel to hear some important words addressed to those who grieve. These words, coming straight from the mouth of Jesus before he died on the Cross, remind us that there is more to life than the time we spend on earth.

While there's no denying that the death of a loved one can be extremely painful to those left behind, the pain can be lessened somewhat by concentrating on the joy that awaits us in heaven. The purpose of this chapter is not to deny the emptiness caused by the death of someone we love. The pain is real, and there is always a void created when someone dies. By looking at what happened when Jesus met a grieving mother, and by listening to his words about eternal life, however, I'm confident that those who grieve can find hope in the midst of their sorrow. Far from being just a promise that things will be better in the distant future, that hope can invigorate those who grieve and allow them to experience peace in the present moment.

THE FACTS

When Jesus entered the city of Nain, he encountered a funeral procession for a man who had died. This individual was the only son of his widowed mother, which left her in an extremely vulnerable position. When Jesus saw her crying in the midst of the crowd, he had compassion on her and said, "Do not weep" (Lk 7:13). He then touched the frame on which the casket rested, causing the procession to stop. Jesus commanded the deceased man to arise, and the man sat up and began to speak. Finally, he gave the resurrected man to his mother. Quite understandably, the crowd was seized with fear and gave glory to God.

Now, shifting over to John's gospel, let's look at what Jesus said to his disciples before his death. His words give insight into what would happen after his death and provide hope in the midst of the sadness that would soon overtake those closest to him: "A little while, and you will see me no more; again a little while, and you will see me" (Jn 16:16). When the disciples expressed confusion about this message, Jesus responded by saying:

> Truly, truly, I say to you, you will weep and lament, but the world will rejoice; you will be sorrowful, but your sorrow will turn into joy. When a woman is in travail she has sorrow, because her hour has come; but when she is delivered of the child, she no longer remembers the anguish, for joy that a child is born into the world. So you have sorrow now, but I will see you again and your hearts will rejoice, and no one will take your joy from you. (Jn 16:20–22)

Unlike the instance where he comforted a grieving mother who was consumed by present sorrow, here Jesus was preparing his followers for the suffering that they would experience in the future. Because he knew that his path through suffering and death would lead to glory, Jesus was able to speak words of comfort before he died.

Perhaps it did not seem relevant to them at the moment, but it would very soon.

A CLOSER LOOK

Although these two events occur at different points in time, they deliver a powerful message when joined together. When viewed as a whole, the actions and words of Jesus provide hope to those who grieve the death of a loved one. Most importantly, the Lord's words come from a place of authority and are spoken by someone who can make good on his promises.

When Jesus saw the grieving mother in the crowd, Luke writes that he "had compassion on her" (Lk 7:13). That's a critical point that should not be overlooked. Even though the woman was in the middle of a crowd and there was a lot going on, Jesus noticed her and was moved with pity because of her situation. Even more importantly, he took action to alleviate her suffering.

As a widow living two thousand years ago, this woman was basically helpless. She would have depended on her only son to provide for her material needs. Therefore, her grief is compounded by the fact that she now has no one to provide for her. Without being asked, Jesus intervenes and offers words of consolation ("Do not weep," Lk 7:13) followed by words of action ("Young man, I say to you, arise," Lk 7:14). As a result, the woman receives her son back. Although it's not explicitly mentioned, we can safely assume that she receives her joy back as well.

Now, let's focus on the words Jesus spoke to his disciples on the night before he died. He begins in a very matter-of-fact way by alluding to the fact that he will be leaving them shortly (via his death), followed by the promise of a reunion at some unspecified time in the future. Understandably, the disciples do not comprehend his message, which gives Jesus the opportunity to elaborate.

As he speaks, the same compassion extended to the widow becomes apparent once again. Jesus knows that his death will cause his friends to grieve, so he proactively attempts to ease their future suffering. In no way does he attempt to downplay their pain ("Truly, truly, I say to you, you will weep and lament," Jn 16:20), but he acknowledges that sorrow for what it is: grief caused by the absence of a loved one.

After acknowledging the reality of their suffering, however, Jesus points to the promise of a future free from sadness ("Your sorrow will turn into joy," Jn 16:20). He doesn't promise when the change will occur, but he does promise that it will. Furthermore, this future joy will occur when they see him again ("I will see you again and your hearts will rejoice," Jn 16:22), and it cannot be taken away by anyone or anything ("No one will take your joy from you," Jn 16:22). Sounds to me like something worth waiting for, don't you think?

WHY IT MATTERS

I'm not going to lie and tell you that life will be the same without your deceased loved one. It won't. They were an irreplaceable gift from God, and your grief is a reaction to the void created by their death. Your life without them will be different. That being said, however, Jesus can and will fill you with a gradually increasing level of peace if you let him. That peace is rooted in our belief that life continues after death, and our hope of a future reunion with our loved ones in heaven.

Before we continue, let's look at how the Church articulates the final realities we all will face: "Each man receives his eternal retribution in his immortal soul at the very moment of his death, in a particular judgment that refers his life to Christ: either entrance into the blessedness of heaven—through a purification or immediately—or immediate and everlasting damnation" (*CCC*, 1022). I'd like to tell you that your deceased loved one is definitely in heaven right now, but I cannot do that. In addition to the possibility of eternal damnation in hell (due to a rejection of God on earth), the Church teaches that a temporary purification process (purgatory) can be necessary before we arrive at our final destination of heaven. I can tell you, however, that you have every reason to be filled with hope that your loved one is in a better place and that you will be reunited with them again one day.

In his farewell address to his disciples, Jesus spoke of a temporary sadness caused by death followed by the

When You're Grieving the Death of a Loved One (Widow of Nain)

promise of a future reunion. Although the joy of heaven isn't an absolute guarantee (every person has free will and can choose to reject God), we have reason to believe that we will experience it. Because God is merciful and wants everyone to be saved (2 Pt 3:9), we can be confident that he will do whatever is possible to make it occur. Because of his faithfulness and love, we know that the Lord will never stop trying to reach those who may be headed toward eternal damnation. When a loved one dies, we can take comfort in knowing that they are now in the Lord's capable and loving hands. He loves them and desires their salvation even more than you do. Furthermore, they are now free from the suffering, temptations, and frustrations of this fallen world.

By all means, continue to pray and offer sacrifices for your deceased loved ones, but don't allow your heart to become troubled with worries about where they may be. Focus instead on the Lord's infinite mercy and love. His desire to live with us forever was so strong that he willingly died on the Cross to open up the gates of heaven. That's the kind of person we can trust with the lives of our loved ones. Even if we can no longer see them or speak with them, we can safely conclude that they are in good hands.

Jesus had pity on the grieving mother, raised her son from the dead, and reunited them. While that reunion will probably not happen for us in this life, we can reasonably believe that it will happen one day. If you are mourning right now, Jesus is aware of your plight. Just as he noticed the widow in the crowd and took steps to alleviate her suffering, he wants to do the same for you.

I once heard it said that we'll be separated from our deceased loved ones for a much shorter time than we'll spend with them in heaven. When you think about it, even fifty years is nothing when compared with eternity. It may be hard to wait, but just imagine how great it will be once that joyful and unending reunion happens. Focusing on that reunion, even if it won't occur for some time, can be enough to make today's burden a little lighter.

PRAYER

Dear Jesus, I am grieving the death of someone I love, and it's not easy. Losing them has created a hole in my life. Things just aren't the same. I'm so sad that I sometimes feel as if I don't want to go on without them. You restored the joy of the woman who lost her son, and I'm asking you to do the same for me. Please be merciful to the one I love, and make it possible for us to be reunited one day. Just knowing that it's possible makes me feel better. Thank you, Jesus. Amen.

DISCUSSION QUESTIONS

1. Read the story of the widow and her son in Luke 7:11–17. What caused Jesus to intervene in the woman's situation? What conclusions can you draw about Jesus from this, and how do those ideas affect you?

2. What has caused (or is causing) you the most grief in dealing with the death of a loved one? How can Jesus help you with that sorrow?

3. Do the words of Jesus in John 16:16–24 affect your feelings about death in any way? Do they make you feel better, worse, or no different? Discuss.

Chapter 15

WHEN YOU JUST DON'T UNDERSTAND (JOB)

Job 42:1-6

As I wrote in the introduction, my goal for this book is to provide examples of God working for good in bad situations, which gives us hope that he can do the same for us. While I am confident that the book's explorations will accomplish the objective in many cases, it would be unfair to overlook situations when this kind of trust feels out of reach. When you're the one suffering, it's not always easy to find comfort by looking at how God worked in the lives of others. After all, this is your problem, and you're the one who is hurting. You may be at the point where you're still unable to see any good coming out of your particular situation.

For that reason, I decided to end this book with the story of the biblical figure whose name is synonymous with suffering: Job. The story of what happened in his life is familiar to many, and he is often used as an example of how to suffer well. For the purposes of this book, however, Job's journey will not be our main focus. It's hardly a secret that Job endured tremendous suffering, made worse by a wife who didn't support him and friends who continually proclaimed that he was responsible for his plight. Therefore, we'll gloss over most of the well-known details and concentrate on something that is recorded in the very last chapter of the book of Job.

Job originally accepted his bad fortune as coming from the hand of a loving God, but eventually he began to question God's judgment. As question after question poured forth from the mouth of Job, God remained silent until he was ready to speak. And boy, did he ever speak!

Maybe you're feeling like Job right now and just can't see how God is doing anything good in your life. If you're not there now, you'll probably be there at some point in the future. Maybe you know someone who is trying to make sense of the senseless. Whatever the case, I believe you'll benefit from examining the dialogue between God and Job. After the Lord spoke, Job finally realized something that he was overlooking. He discovered the secret to finding peace when everything is going wrong. It's a concept that Paul understood when he penned Romans 8:28. Although it's not complicated, it may be the most powerful lesson in this book. Let's eavesdrop on a life-changing conversation between God and Job. I know that they won't mind.

When You Just Don't Understand (Job)

THE FACTS

Job, a man who lived in the land of Uz, was described in the Bible as being "blameless and upright" (Jb 1:1). He was someone who feared God and avoided evil. He had many possessions and servants, plus seven sons and three daughters. With God's permission, Satan set out to tempt Job, believing that his goodness could be attributed to his many blessings. The evil one believed that Job would end up cursing God if all that he had was taken away.

The first chapter of the book of Job sees him losing his property and children, but he "did not sin" or blame God in response. Job reacted to these catastrophic events by speaking words that reveal just how much he trusted in the Lord: "Naked I came from my mother's womb, and naked shall I return; the LORD gave, and the LORD has taken away; blessed be the name of the LORD" (Jb 1:21).

After enduring physical afflictions and the harassment of his friends (who claimed that all of these calamities were brought on by his hidden sinfulness), Job eventually broke down and questioned the Lord's actions: "If I sin, what do I do to you, you watcher of men? Why have you made me your mark? Why have I become a burden to you?" (Jb 7:20).

For the next several chapters, we hear a series of conversations between Job and his friends. Through all of the accusations, questioning, and explanations, however, God remains silent. Finally, in chapter 38 we hear God speak. Instead of answering Job's questions, God asks some questions of his own. For the next four chapters, Job is bombarded with a series of questions that were designed to drive home the point that God's wisdom is infinitely greater than ours. It worked. In the final chapter of the book of Job, we get to hear Job's response to the Lord's questions. To paraphrase them would be an injustice. Here is what Job said:

> I know that you can do all things, and that no purpose of yours can be thwarted. "Who is this that hides counsel without knowledge?" Therefore I have uttered what I did not understand, things too wonderful for me, which I did not know. "Hear, and I will speak; I will question you, and you declare to me." I had heard of you by the hearing of the ear, but now my eye sees you; therefore I despise myself, and repent in dust and ashes. (Jb 42:2–6)

As the book closes with this lesson in hand, we're informed that Job's fortune was restored and he ended up with twice as much as he had before. He would go on to have seven more sons and three more daughters. Finally, Job died "an old man, and full of days" (Jb 42:17).

A CLOSER LOOK

When the Bible introduces us to Job, he seems like a faith-filled rock star. Not only are we informed of his righteousness, but we see it in action. Even losing his family and

When You Just Don't Understand (Job)

possessions isn't enough to make him question God. Little by little, however, he gets beaten down by his friends and circumstances and begins to demand answers from the Lord.

What I find noteworthy in this story is that God isn't in a hurry to answer Job. For most of the book, Job and his friends do all the talking, and God is silent. As we'll see when he does decide to answer, God's silence didn't mean that he wasn't listening. He knew everything that was said, as evidenced by his response. That's an important lesson for those of us who sometimes accuse the Lord of not hearing our prayers. He always hears our prayers, but he answers in his own time.

Over time, Job allows himself to be overcome by bad advice and unfavorable circumstances. His once-strong faith has been weakened, and he begins to question God's judgment. For the first time, Job begins to ask "why?" It's a question I have found myself asking many times. Typically, this happens when I look at God's actions through the lens of my imperfect and limited human intellect. To put it bluntly, it occurs when I forget that God is God and I am not.

Ultimately, when the time is right, God addresses Job. What is interesting, however, is that God doesn't answer any of Job's questions. Instead, God goes on the offensive and asks Job more than fifty questions of his own. Every one of these questions is designed to remind Job of who is the Creator and who is the creature.

The Lord may not have answered any of Job's questions directly, but that doesn't mean that he didn't answer. Job's response and subsequent repentance illustrates that he heard the answer loud and clear. Job finally remembered an important piece of information that he knew when we were first introduced to him, but had forgotten somewhere in the midst of his suffering: God is infinitely wiser than we are. His actions may seem illogical to us, but that's because he's God and we're not. It was a long and painful process, but Job finally figured it out. Hopefully, looking at his story will help us to do the same.

WHY IT MATTERS

As soon as I started writing this book, I made the decision to end with the story of Job. I chose to include his story not because of the tremendous suffering Job endured or the faithful example he set, but because of a valuable lesson he learned in the end. It's the perfect parting lesson to share with you as we bring this book to a close. No matter how many different ways you see God working good in bad situations, it's very likely that you will run into a situation one day where that kind of faith feels beyond you. That's precisely when the last chapter of Job becomes invaluable.

Just like Job, we will all encounter circumstances in life that don't make sense. It may involve a sudden death, unexpected job loss, or an unanswered prayer. No matter how hard we pray or seek answers, we get nothing in return. In some cases, even biblical examples of God's provision aren't enough to bring us comfort. When this happens, the Lord is extending the same offer he extended to Job: "Trust me." It's an offer that can't be accepted if everything makes sense to us. The only time we can choose this path of unconditional trust is when we are so immersed in darkness that we must operate solely on faith. In the end, that's what Job did. If you're still struggling to see a ray of light in the darkness of your situation, there's a good possibility that God is offering you what he offered Job: a chance to trust him in a radical way.

PRAYER

Dear Father, no matter how hard I try, I just don't understand why this is happening to me. Even the biblical stories of how you brought good from evil aren't helping me. I just can't see any good coming from my present situation. My repeated questions to you have gone unanswered. In many ways, I feel like Job, only with less faith. Please increase my faith so that I can find the comfort he found. Help me to trust you even though I don't understand. I ask this in the name of Jesus. Amen.

DISCUSSION QUESTIONS

1. In the book of Job, God is silent for the first thirty-seven chapters. Why do you think that is? How can the Lord's silence benefit us?

2. In the end, Job only received one indirect answer from God to all of his questions: "Because I'm God and you're not!" Why is that answer more helpful to Job than all of the answers that he didn't receive?

3. Why do you think we often can't be at peace until God answers our questions? What does that reveal about us? What does that reveal about God?

Conclusion

BELIEVING IS SEEING

A few years ago, I was speaking in West Chester, Pennsylvania, and referenced Romans 8:28 in my talk. Just as I have done throughout this book, I made the point that God can always bring good out of any situation. Or to put it another way: everything will work out for the best if we give God a chance. After the talk, I was answering questions from the audience, and a woman asked me a sincere and reasonable question: "What about when things *don't* work out for the best?"

She wasn't angry or trying to cause problems, but was just trying to understand a concept that can be very difficult to comprehend. When I asked her to elaborate, she explained that both her husband and her son had died. She had prayed for them to be healed from their illnesses, but that did not happen. In her mind, even though she had turned to God for help, things did not work out for the best.

I did my best to answer delicately and honestly, leaning heavily on the story of Job. I explained that, more than anything else, God is concerned with our eternal salvation. He wants to ensure that we navigate the pitfalls of this life so that we can live with him forever. Sometimes this requires him to act in a way that we don't like or understand. While it may not be pleasant and most of us would do anything to avoid it, suffering has a way of purifying us and drawing us closer to God. As a result, the "unanswered" prayers and resulting suffering that can cause us to question God's goodness and love are sometimes exactly what we need to get to heaven. Once again turning to the wisdom of Paul, we are invited to consider that the unpleasant circumstances in life are not barriers to God's love, and that through these experiences, God is drawing us to an even greater good than we can imagine. As Paul wrote, "For I am sure that neither death, nor life, nor angels, nor principalities, nor things present, nor things to come, nor powers, nor height, nor depth, nor anything else in all creation, will be able to separate us from the love of God in Christ Jesus our Lord" (Rom 8:38–39).

While it still may not be easy to accept, learning to think like this can be very comforting. Even when we can't perceive God's love through our senses, we can work backward and adopt the conviction that everything that happens can draw us more deeply into God's love. In order to choose to believe this, however, it's necessary to cast aside the old adage that "seeing is believing" and replace it with a new one: "believing is seeing." If we embrace Paul's philosophy that "in everything God works for good with those who love him" (Rom 8:28) and view life's circumstances through that lens, it becomes easier to see what we already believe. It takes practice, surrender, and humility, but choosing to believe in God's goodness and power no matter what happens can bring us great peace in any situation.

Throughout this book, we have looked at biblical stories of God bringing good in bad situations. As I stated in the introduction, my hope is that you would be able to look at these examples and discover ways that God is working for good in your own difficult situation. You may see it immediately, but it typically takes some time. I encourage you to keep looking, as God often works in very small and subtle ways.

It's also possible that, no matter how hard you pray or seek, the only answer you'll receive is the one God gave to Job. It sounds harsh, but it can also be extremely comforting. Like Job, if we get to the point where we're content to "let God be God," we can end up living a peaceful life. I'm not there yet myself, but I'm working on it.

In closing, I'd like you to know that I'm praying for you. If I offended you in any way or somehow trivialized your suffering, I'm sorry. My intent was to bring you comfort by pointing to concrete examples of how the Lord worked in the lives of others. I tried to choose stories that represent a variety of different situations. In each of these cases, God can be seen working for good. Even though I may not know or understand the details of your situation,

I do know what it's like to look at the circumstances in my life, then look at God and say, "Huh?"

I don't know if any of us will be able to achieve Paul's level of understanding, but I do believe that we can move closer to it. There's a psalm that was undoubtedly known and prayed by Saul the Pharisee (before he was known as Paul). It's one that has helped me many times when I was trying to make sense of the senseless. Traditionally, these words are attributed to King David and represent someone who has chosen to leave the big details up to God. There's a great deal of peace to be found when we choose to trust God and not attempt to figure out everything that he does. I feel that it's fitting to end the book with these words.

PSALM 131

O Lord, my heart is not lifted up,
    my eyes are not raised too high;
I do not occupy myself with things
    too great and too marvelous for me.
But I have calmed and quieted my soul,
    like a child quieted at its mother's breast;
    like a child that is quieted is my soul.
O Israel, hope in the Lord
    from this time forth and for evermore.

Gary Zimak is a Catholic speaker and the best-selling author of a number of books, including *Give Up Worry for Lent!*, *Let Go of Anger and Stress!*, *Give Up Worry for Good!*, and *Let Go of Your Fear*.

He is the host of *The Gary Zimak Show* and the podcast *Following the Truth*. He previously served as director of parish services at Mary, Mother of the Redeemer Catholic Church in North Wales, Pennsylvania, and as the host of *Spirit in the Morning* on Holy Spirit Radio in Philadelphia. He is a frequent speaker and retreat leader at Catholic parishes and conferences across the country.

His work has appeared in *Catholic Digest*, the *National Catholic Register*, *Catholic Exchange*, *Catholic Philly*, and *Catholic Answers Magazine*. Zimak has been a guest on numerous television and radio programs, including EWTN's *Bookmark* and *Women of Grace*, *Catholic Answers Live*, *Morning Air*, and the *Son Rise Morning Show*.

Zimak earned a bachelor of science degree in business administration from Drexel University.

He lives in Mount Laurel, New Jersey, with his wife. They have two children.

www.followingthetruth.com
Facebook: Gary.Zimak.speaker.author
Twitter: @gary_zimak

MORE BY GARY ZIMAK

Give Up Worry for Lent!
40 Days to Finding Peace in Christ

In *Give Up Worry for Lent!*, Gary Zimak offers fellow worriers practical, scripture-centered advice on how to relinquish the need to control the uncontrollable—not just for Lent but for good—and how to find peace in Christ.

Give Up Worry for Good!
8 Weeks to Hopeful Living and Lasting Peace

This eight-week resource can be used any time of year and will teach you how to get rid of the stressful, energy-sapping behaviors that keep you on edge and rob you of joy.

Let Go of Anger and Stress!
Be Transformed by the Fruits of the Spirit

Using the nine fruits of the Spirit as a guide, Gary Zimak will help you to bear good fruit when you're dealing with anger to help you find peace and to live the life God has planned for you.

Let Go of Your Fear
Choosing to Trust Jesus in Life's Stormy Times

Gary Zimak explores two Gospel stories of Jesus calming storms—and his disciples—to show you how to manage the big feelings of fear in your life.

Look for these titles wherever books and eBooks are sold.
Visit **avemariapress.com** for more information.